HANDBOOK OF
CHURCH
DISCIPLINE

Resources by Jay E. Adams

The Christian Counselor's Manual
The Christian Counselor's Casebook
The Competent to Counsel
Handbook of Church Discipline
How to Help People Change
Marriage, Divorce, and Remarriage in the Bible
Preaching with Purpose
Shepherding God's Flock
Solving Marriage Problems
A Theology of Christian Counseling

HANDBOOK OF CHURCH DISCIPLINE

A Right and Privilege of
Every Church Member

JAY E. ADAMS

ZONDERVAN

Handbook of Church Discipline
Copyright © 1874, 1986 by Jay E. Adams

Requests for information should be addressed to:
Zondervan, 3900 *Sparks Dr. SE, Grand Rapids, Michigan* 49546

Library of Congress Cataloging-in-Publication Data

Adams, Jay Edward.
      Handbook of church discipline.
      (The Jay Adams library)
      Includes indexes.
      ISBN: 978-0-310-51191-5
      1. Church discipline—Handbooks, manuals, etc.   I. Title.
  II. Adams, Jay Edward. Jay Adams library.
  BV740.A34   1986
  262.9   86-23574

Unless otherwise indicated all New Testament quotations are from the Christian
Counselor's New Testament.

Edited by Joan Johnson
Designed by Louise Bauer

Printed in the United States of America

Contents

Preface

This book in your hand is just what it calls itself—a handbook. It is not a collection of anecdotes, nor an academically oriented tome that discusses the scholarly aspects of the subject. No. It is a handbook for you— for busy pastors and Christian workers who want to understand and faithfully carry out the task of church discipline. I have three objectives in view:

1. To present a clear, concise biblical description of church discipline. This book is designed to acquaint you with the major facts delineated in the Scriptures concerning the purpose and the process of discipline. The first objective, therefore, is to help you acquire a working knowledge of biblical church discipline.

2. To provide a ready reference to which you may turn for help in situations requiring church discipline. I have purposely kept the book as slim as possible. Besides the index, I have also strategically placed section headings throughout to make it maximally useful.

3. To convince the dubious that church discipline is not only a biblical requirement (and therefore

feasible) but also a right and privilege of every member of the church of Christ, and therefore, a blessing that should not be withheld. This book is intended to encourage church leaders to reinstate—or introduce—the practice of church discipline in their congregations.

Much of the material has been presented orally at seminars of the Christian Legal Society and at various pastors' meetings. It has been developed to meet the needs expressed at these gatherings. In part, I have written to meet a demand that these lectures be put in written form.

If, in any measure, the three objectives mentioned above are achieved as a fruit of this book, I shall be grateful. As I think of the homes that have been hopelessly broken, the estrangements that have permanently resulted, and the misery that has been unnecessarily caused by the failure of churches to practice church discipline, or to practice it biblically, my heart aches. Even more tragically, as I consider the ruins of many congregations torn by schismatic and factious persons who have been allowed to wreak havoc with Christ's flock, and the sickness of many others weakened by the infectious toxin of unrepentant sin that circulates in Christ's body of believers, I am deeply moved. And above all, as I think of the dishonor that has been heaped upon the name of our Lord because of the tarnished witness of churches that harbor glaring violators of His holy commandments, I am appalled.

May God use you to be one of those who in our time ministers His Word effectively to heal hurts, strengthen Christ's people, and bring honor to His name through church discipline!

Introduction

Mary has left Bill and announces to him she is going to divorce. Mr. and Mrs. Jones are taking the elders out for dinner each Sunday, trying to persuade them that they should withdraw the congregation from its present denomination to join another. After a loud and protracted argument, Sally and Jane have declared that they do not care to speak to one another again; it has been four weeks since the fight and they refuse to reconcile. Peggy knows she is pregnant out of wedlock. Harry has discovered that the church organist is a homosexual. What do all of these people have in common? In one way or another, they all need the blessings and the benefits of church discipline.

But if they belong to the average church, none, or at best few of them, would be able to profit from the healing, purifying balm of discipline. And discipline, in such churches, would not be considered a blessing or benefit, but an outmoded relic of the Dark Ages, unsuitable to a modern congregation. That is the tragedy of the church of our time.

Many of you who are pastors, elders, and church

leaders know that your own congregation is remiss in the exercise of church discipline. Perhaps you say, "Well, it is so far gone, there isn't much hope of reestablishing it in my church." Or, possibly, in frustration you reply, "Sure, I know we ought to have church discipline, but I wouldn't know where to begin. Besides that, I don't even know how to exercise discipline; they didn't teach me anything about that in seminary."

For all such persons—for the uninitiated in ministry and for the experienced who see a need to be more biblically effective in church discipline—this book is written. To the timid, to the confused, to the willing but ignorant, I say, there is hope. You *can* indeed institute, reinstitute, or strengthen church discipline in your congregation.

How do I know that is true? Because the Lord Jesus Himself set forth the basic principles of church discipline, because He who stands amid the lampstands cares about your church and wants you to practice discipline. Whatever He requires of His people He gives both the wisdom and the strength to do. That is why I say it is possible to have discipline in your congregation; yes, in *your* congregation, if it is a church where the Word of God is preached and where, in spite of many irregularities, beneath all there is a fundamental desire to please the Lord.

There are many congregations across the land in which church discipline is being revived: this is a most encouraging sign. Indeed, it is evidence that the recent surge in evangelical thought and concern extends deeper than many have supposed. Since discipline is a primary means available for drawing a line between the church and the world, one of the chief ways of identifying God's people, and a pivotal element in distinguishing a true church from a false one, it is of utmost importance to reestablish good discipline in this period in which there has been much confusion in determining the true churches of Christ. Moreover, in the biblical counseling revival, those involved have discovered that church discipline is an essential tool. Indeed, it is this revival that has spurred the new interest in church discipline. Without it there is no way to bring many counseling cases to a satisfactory end. With discipline all cases can be resolved. That interest, of course, views church discipline from the counselor's perspective. It thinks of discipline in its narrower sense as a tool for counseling. Looking at discipline from another, broader viewpoint, counseling may be thought of as an essential part of the processes of church discipline. Both perspectives are valid and important. But either way you look at it—and we shall consider the matter from both sides in this book—counseling and church discipline are inextricably intertwined; neither can be carried on effectively and biblically without the other.

Much more could be said about church discipline in this introduction by tracing its course down through the ages or by showing how it was used for the wrong purposes in harsh and harmful ways and how, in reaction, it was laid aside. It could be shown that this, in turn, led to the easy takeover of the mainline evangelical churches by liberals who, because the practice of church discipline had been abandoned, were able to espouse their heretical teaching with so little opposition. It could be shown that much of the weakened state of the churches in the present time is the direct result of a failure in church discipline. Divorces occur, church splits take place, false teaching is introduced and the like, because the means Christ outlined for forestalling such things, the process and application of church discipline, is no longer intact. But, having simply said that much, let us move on.

One of the greatest tragedies resulting from the failure of church discipline is the wreckage of homes strewn across the land. Had discipline been in place and properly functioning, few of the marriage failures and the child/parent problems now facing the church would have occurred. They would have been nipped in the bud by lively, loving disciplinary action, dealt with summarily, and in most cases, coupled with good biblical counseling (which, remember, is an essential element in effective church discipline) would have been put to rest. Failure of church discipline as a viable function has led to chaos in the church. And this chaos, in turn, has led to every other form of difficulty and trouble.

From what I have said, you can see how important church discipline is, can't you? Indeed, the work of the church cannot be (indeed, is not being) conducted properly apart from church discipline.

"Well, then, what is church discipline, and how shall we go about establishing and practicing it?" you ask. I shall try to give you adequate and satisfying scriptural answers to those two questions.

I consider myself qualified to write about this matter only because over the last twenty-five years, in one way or another, I have been forced to face most of the issues connected with church discipline as I have pastored churches, taught and practiced counseling, and dealt with case after case in question-and-answer sessions at pastors' conferences. These endeavors have driven me to the Scriptures for God's answers, and while I may not have all of them, I think that I have enough to help you get biblical church discipline under way and functioning well in your congregation. At least that is my desire and my prayer. You will have to judge whether or not I have succeeded.

1

What Is Church Discipline?

The terms "disciple" and "discipline" obviously have a common Latin source. The source is a word family that has to do with education. Discipline is inextricably linked to education.

But the kind of education of which the Bible speaks, and from which church discipline takes its impetus, is very different from the sort of education with which we are now familiar in America. The educational model from which the idea of church discipline stems once was known in our country, but it became extinct as the result of the successful spread of the permissive, self-expression practices advocated by John Dewey and others in an earlier generation. Biblical education, from which ideas of church discipline flow, is education with teeth; it is education that sees to it that the job gets done.[1]

---

[1] I can remember once upon a time my schoolmates and me singing, "School days, school days, good old golden rule days;

The Old Testament word *musar* and the New Testament word *paideia* set forth this idea of education backed by force. As Hebrews 12:5–11 makes clear (here the New Testament writer uses *paideia* to translate the Hebrew *musar* into Greek), such education is not always pleasant and at the time can be quite painful:

> Of course, all discipline (*paideia*) seems painful rather than pleasant for the moment, but later on it yields the peaceful fruit of righteousness to those who have been trained by it (Hebrews 12:11).

But notice the purpose of discipline: it functions in the educational process to produce righteousness as its fruit, a fruit which, when you bite into it, tastes like peace.

Righteousness (rightness; conformity to Christ's standard of conduct) has the flavor of peace because, wherever it is found, it produces harmony and order. Where there is conformity to God's will, there is structure; where there is biblical structure the prime condition for learning is present: peace.

Without peace, learning is impossible. Education depends on order. That is one of the major reasons why in the recent past, and even up to the present, there has been such poor learning in our schools— peace, a chief factor in the learning situation, has been missing. Where there is no peace, there is no learning; where there is no discipline, there is no order; where there is no order there is no peace. Discipline is, at its heart and core, good order.

But why should we be thinking about education? How is it that church discipline connects with education? Because the very term that Christ uses concern-

reading and writing and 'rithmetic, taught to the tune of a hickory stick . . . " What could be more foreign to today's public schools?

ing the church indicates that He conceives of it as an educational institution. When Jesus beckons to us, inviting us to find refreshment in Him, He does so in educational language:

> Come to Me, all who labor and are heavily burdened, and I will refresh you (the word in the original is a verb, not a noun, as the KJV has it).
> Put My yoke on you and learn from Me; I am meek and humble in heart, and you will discover refreshment for your souls.
> My yoke is easy to wear and My burden is light.
> (Matthew 11:28–30)

Here the great Teacher describes conversion as the experience of enrolling in His school and learning how to live from Him. Conversion involves becoming a *disciple* (student) of Christ. One does not take some six-week course to qualify for entrance into the church, graduate from the course, and cease being a student. No, there is nothing like that in the Bible. Rather, the entire course of one's Christian life is described as a learning experience in the school of Christ.

Notice the educational language in Christ's invitation: "learn from Me," "Put My yoke on you." The latter expression was used by the Jews to describe one's submission to a teacher as he became his disciple (cf. Lamentations 3:27; Sirach 51:23–26; 6:24). In Sirach 51:23, 26, for instance, we read, "Draw near to me, you who are untaught, and lodge in my school. . . . Put your neck under the yoke, and let your sons receive instruction. . . ." (*Apocrypha*, RSV).

Moreover, when Jesus gave what is called the "Great Commission," He really issued a command to recruit students for His school. Again, we meet educational language throughout: "disciple (recruit and train students from) all nations, . . . teaching them to observe . . ." (Matthew 28:18, 20). When we are baptized into the church, we thereby matriculate into Christ's school. Then, for the rest of our earthly life, we are to be taught (not facts alone, but also) to obey the commands of Christ. This is education with force, education backed up by the discipline of good order that is necessary for learning to take place. And of those recalcitrant students who grow restive under His tutelage, Jesus says, "I convict and discipline these about whom I care" (Revelation 3:19a).

If when the preacher says, "Let me read from God's Word, . . ." only some listen, but others walk down the aisle to the collection plate and put their money in, some go outside for a break, some sing a hymn, some start talking, and some begin praying, you have chaos. Suppose the same disorder continued throughout the sermon. There would be precious little learning occurring![2] In the church service all things must be done "decently and in order" (1 Corinthians 14:40); various rules for order and discipline in the conduct of worship are given in the chapter.

But what is true of the church service is also true of the entire life of the church as a body. All must be done with order and decency. God will have no chaos in His church (cf. 1 Thessalonians 4:11; 2 Thessalonians 3:6, 11). In the last verse of the preceding parenthesis, Paul speaks of those "among you who are living in a totally *unstructured* way" and writes some strong words, to which we shall return later, about how to discipline them if they fail to heed His orders.

So, God is running a school in which He expects learning to take place. To bring about that learning,

---

[2] This is probably the sort of thing that Paul was describing in 1 Corinthians 14:26, when he speaks of everybody interested in "doing his own thing."

He has ordered His church to enforce strict rules of discipline. That she has failed to do so in recent days accounts for much of the ignorance and gullibility found among so many Christians in our time. If words from the pulpit are not enforced by action from the congregation and the elders, members will learn that the church does not really mean what it says. They may learn facts for the next Bible quiz, but not how to "observe" (obey) Christ's commands.

Discipline brings "peace." That is another reason why there is much unrest in many congregations, homes, and lives. Where there is chaos rather than the disciplined, structured, orderly living that comes when a church enforces Christ's commands, unrest of every sort arises. And the irony is that, apart from church discipline, there is no way to settle it down. One finds rest, refreshment, and peace in Christ's school only when learning is enforced through His rules of order.

Thus, discipline is not, as many have thought, simply the negative task of reading troublemakers out of the church. Rather, first above all, it is God's provision for good order in His church that creates conditions for the instruction and growth of the members. Discipline has a positive function.

As you can see already from the few references cited, discipline is not an option, something that "might be nice if we decide we want it." It is commanded by Christ and is, therefore, the right and privilege of every student. How can a student be expected to learn to observe Christ's commands in the midst of an undisciplined, disorderly, unstructured congregation? He can't. When he enters such a harum-scarum situation as exists in so many churches today, he is immediately deprived of his Christ-given right to learn in a truly educational atmosphere. It is time that we recognized the importance of discipline to good order and learning in the church. Today we talk a lot about church growth; but growth is impossible in the lives of members apart from church discipline.

While the positive purpose of discipline that grows out of its educational emphasis is good order, it is also the case that this good order leads to the honor of God, the welfare of the church, and where possible, the reclamation of the offender.

The honor of God is a consistent theme throughout the Bible. We see the necessity for discipline in the Old Testament, even before a formal church was organized as such. Abraham pointed out to Lot that it was not proper for their herdsmen to fight over the watering holes and the grazing territory, because, as Moses noted, "the Canaanite and the Perizzite were then living in the land" (Genesis 13:5–8). God's name would be besmirched before the heathen. That emphasis persists throughout the Bible.

The welfare of the church is at stake when there is need for discipline. If 1 Corinthians 5 teaches anything, it teaches that. The leaven was to be cleaned out; the undisciplined offender was to be put out of the church for his refusal to repent of his sin lest his influence for evil permeate the whole.[3] Already many were acting arrogantly (v. 2) and even boasting of their liberal-mindedness (v. 6).

Moreover, the consistent theme of church discipline is concern for the offender.[4] His repentance and

---

[3] White/Blue, in their book *Healing the Wounded* (Downers Grove, Ill.: InterVarsity Press, 1985), pp. 65–66, are surely wrong when they differ from the interpretation that equates cleaning out the leaven with removing the offender (v. 2), delivering him to Satan (v. 5), and putting him out of the midst (v. 13).

[4] Remember Christ's words in Revelation 3:19, "I convict and discipline those about whom I care" (*philo*). He does this through

reclamation are always to be a hoped-for expectation, and much of the effort expended in properly conducted discipline is directed toward that end. That goal is expressed clearly in Matthew 18:15ff. and in 1 Corinthians 5:5. And, as we shall see in a chapter later on, the restoration of an offender should be made a joyous occasion of great importance to the church.

So, church discipline is not only required and necessary to the good order of a church that bears Christ's name, but it is the source of peace in the church leading to learning and every other good thing. God is honored by church discipline, rightly administered, and is greatly dishonored by its absence. How often is the unbeliever able to sneer at the church, to its shame, saying of one of its undisciplined members, "He's a deacon in the church, but they do nothing about him in spite of the well-known fact that he runs around with women and gets drunk."

Problems between members and in homes often are quickly resolved by church discipline, but they persist and get worse when it is not applied. When did you last hear someone say, "I've done *everything* to save my marriage," when, in fact, the person has done virtually nothing? The spouse has not even initiated the first steps of discipline set forth in Matthew 18, because no one ever told him to do so and he has never seen such a thing happen in his congregation. Discipline is important, then, and cannot be dismissed so readily as it has been without great peril to the church, to the offender, and of greatest importance, to the name of Christ.

His Word (cf. 2 Timothy 3:16, where "convicting" and "disciplining" are said to be two of the four "uses" of Scripture).

2

Preventive Discipline

We have seen that etymologically the word "discipline" is related to the Latin words *disco* ("to learn") and *disciplina* ("learning"), having to do with education. And we have seen that discipline may be defined as the functions of a school that promote and maintain conditions of learning together with those that root out all hindrances to it.

You will have noticed in that definition two parts: (1) positively, functions that promote and maintain conditions of learning, and (2) negatively, functions that root out all hindrances to the conditions of learning. The prime condition of learning with which discipline is involved is the righteousness that leads to peace. Where there is righteousness (good order, in conformity with God's requirements and truth), there is peace; where there is peace, learning can take place. And when discipline is intact, God's name is honored, His church grows, and offenders against God and His righteousness are reclaimed in repentance. That is what discipline is all about.

But too often discipline is thought of only in a remedial sense; its promotional and preventive aspects are unrecognized or ignored. The remedial side of discipline, like the proverbial squeaky wheel, gets all the grease. Parents have a tendency only to complain when a child does wrong; they tend to forget to compliment when a child does well. It is easier to complain than to compliment because you must think to do the latter; occasions for complaint call attention to themselves. So too is it with discipline. We do not tend to think about the discipline of good order in faith and practice, in individual lives, or in the life of the corporate body, because good discipline is unobtrusive; instead, we focus on the sensational—the cases of discipline where dramatic, sinful events occur and excommunication or putting out of the church may take place.[1] But that is a mistake. And it is the purpose of this chapter to call attention to the positive effects of good order, peace, and purity in the church as they promote the glory of God.

Discipline is, therefore, a two-edged sword that has a preventive side and a corrective side. But both prevention and correction have to do with doctrine and with life. Preventive discipline involves teaching truth in such a way that it promotes godliness. It means "teaching to observe." It is concerned not merely with facts, but rather with facts transformed into life and ministry. When Christians are fed a regular diet of truth from the Scriptures in such a way that they grow by it, there will be far less need for remedial discipline in a

---

[1] Excommunication and putting out of the church are not one and the same thing, as we shall have occasion to see *infra*. For now, simply note the distinction and accept that my words in this place are not redundant.

church. Those matters in which one finds himself
straying from the path will be met by the individual
himself or, informally and early on, through the help of
other brothers and sisters in the body, and formal
church discipline will be largely unnecessary. That
ought to be the characteristic and ordinary way in
which discipline functions in the everyday life of a
church.

But even in the best of the apostolic churches,
there were times when discipline had to be carried
further. The church had to become involved, excommunication and cutting the bonds of fellowship had to
take place, and it was even necessary to put people
out of the church (cf. Revelation 2:2).

Crabb's *Synonyms*[2]—an invaluable work for dis-
cerning earlier usages of English words and, consequently, earlier modes of English life and thought that
are exhibited by them—shows that in former times the
word *discipline* carried a more positive connotation;
good order and prevention were its uppermost concern. Rather than comprising it, or for that matter,
being confused with it, *discipline* was clearly distin-
guished from *correction*, a term that was used to refer
to the removal of evils that had actualized. It was only
later that correction was caught up in the English word
discipline.

In more recent times, of course, the preventive
side has almost entirely given way to the corrective.
The history of the facts is recorded in the gradual
evolution of the words involved. Today, say the words
"church discipline" and you will get responses that
have wholly to do with correction. There will be no
thought of good order, good doctrine, and smoothly

[2] George Crabb, *English Synonyms.* (New York: Harper Brothers, 1891), p. 275.

functioning church life. In most minds today, discipline means "the way you get rid of troublemakers."

I have taken the time to emphasize this fact because, until we are able to restore the two-sided, biblical emphasis, we shall go on thinking wrongly and, as a result, acting wrongly about discipline. There will be no wholesale change in practice until there is a wholesale change in concept. And even if corrective discipline alone were restored, it would do much harm because that would lead to its early elimination, as it did in the recent past when the emphasis on correction overshadowed the emphasis on prevention.[3]

What must be reestablished is the full biblical concept of discipline, both preventive and remedial; not merely the one or the other. When either the remedial or corrective side is discussed, its positive aspects—promoting the glory of God, the welfare of the church, and the reclamation of the offender—likewise should be noted. In all its aspects, discipline must be seen as a blessing; it is a privilege of all believers that the church does wrong to withhold from them. Even in its corrective measures, discipline must be shown to be the privilege that it is—the privilege, when necessary, of having the informal care and concern of other members of the body and the care of Christ Himself working formally through the officers of His church, to bring a straying member back into the ways of truth and righteousness.

But it is always difficult to maintain the preventive and positive emphasis when discussing discipline for the very reason already mentioned: the sensational calls attention to itself and tends to crowd out the

---

[3] Part of the problem lies in the fact that during this period all the stress was placed on formal discipline nearly to the exclusion of the informal discipline that individual members of the body are taught in Scripture to practice among themselves.

ordinary, which does not. Yet that in itself is good reason for talking all the more about preventive discipline. Perhaps a more frequent use of the word from the pulpit and in general conversation, when speaking of good order and true belief, would help.[4] Surely we should ever keep before us, and before the minds of the members of our congregations, the fact that the more preventive discipline there is, the less corrective discipline there needs to be.

Preventive discipline, the promotion of good order and true belief, is both the formal responsibility of the leadership of the church—such as the elders, the pastor-teacher, and the deacons—and the informal responsibility of all of the members of the church. Ephesians 4:11–12 makes that clear. The leadership exists to build up the members in their faith and to help them discover, develop, and deploy their gifts for mutual ministry among themselves, so that the whole body builds itself up into the stature of Christ.

All the "one anothering" passages (e.g., Hebrews 10:24–25; Colossians 3:16), in which believers are exhorted to assist one another in various ways according to their gifts and their loving concern for each other, stress the informal aspects of positive, preventive discipline. It is good order, for instance, to love and do fine deeds; and it is informal preventive discipline for believers to "*stimulate* one another" to love and do fine deeds (Hebrews 10:24). It is good order when believers regularly attend the meetings of the body; it is good informal discipline when they *encourage* others to faithful attendance (Hebrews 10:25). These

---

[4]Paul made a point of commending the Colossian church, saying "I am . . . delighted to see your good *order* . . ." (Colossians 2:5). The word here is *taxis.* In 1 Thessalonians 5:14; 2 Thessalonians 3:6–7, 11, Paul condemns those who live an "unstructured" or "disorderly" (*ataktos*) life.

are concrete examples of preventive, positive discipline. But the encouragement of one believer by another to good works does not make the headlines the way that the excommunication of a gay songleader does.

While I should like to spend much time discussing the various ways in which good order may be promoted and maintained among God's people, it would take a book in itself to do so, and the book would have to concern itself with the common interchanges that ought to be going on in any local school of Christ all the time. In other words, all that believers, formally and informally, ought to be doing to promote such faith and practice is a part of positive, preventive discipline. It is both impossible and inappropriate here to attempt to detail such activity.

The important thing, then, is to keep in mind that although in this book the emphasis is on the remedial or corrective side of church discipline—and rightly ought to be, since that is where most of the help and instruction are needed at this point in time—nevertheless, in the actual practice of the local church, the emphasis ought to be on the positive, preventive side.

3

Corrective Discipline

There are five steps in corrective discipline. They may best be understood by careful study of this diagram:

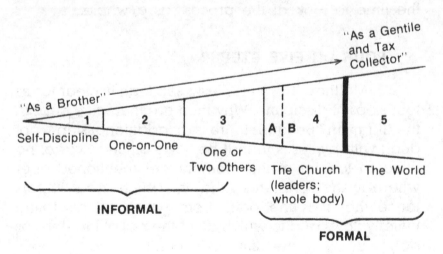

You will notice that the first three steps are informal and do not involve official action by the organized church, but pertain solely to the activities of individual members acting on their own initiative in obedience to Christ's commands. The fourth and the fifth involve the church as an official organization. Moreover, during the first four the offender is regarded as a Christian, but during the fifth he is regarded as an unbeliever.

You will also notice that as discipline progresses from one step to the next, the number of persons participating enlarges (as indicated by the widening of the lines in the diagram), moving from one individual disciplining himself, to a one-on-one confrontation, to calling in one or two others to help, to the assistance of the local church and, finally, to exposure to the world. Each of these factors is of importance and must be explained and elucidated in turn. In the rest of the book I shall do just that, but in this chapter I shall take the time to look at the process as a whole.

FOUR OR FIVE STEPS?

In Matthew 18:15–17, Jesus sets forth in clear terms four steps of discipline. Why then are there five steps in the diagram? Because there is an additional step—not dealt with by Jesus in that passage, since it was of no concern to Him at the moment, yet mentioned elsewhere in the Scriptures—that is of such great importance that it is the point from which all discipline initially flows and to which all of the rest of the steps or stages in discipline ultimately point.

Therefore, I have added in front of the four steps of Matthew 18 a step called "self-discipline." This matter does not arise in Jesus' list of steps, since He is concerned about what to do when there is a matter between brothers (v. 18). He starts one step further along the line. Here is what He said:

> If your brother sins against you, go and convict him of his sin privately, with just the two of you present. If he listens to you, you have won your brother.
>
> But if he won't listen to you, take with you one or two others so that by the mouth of two or three witnesses every word may be confirmed.
>
> And if he refuses to listen to them, tell it to the church. And if he refuses to listen to the church, treat him as a heathen and a tax collector.
>
> (Matthew 18:15–17)

As you can see, Jesus' interest does not extend backward to the struggle in the offender before he commits the offense. But in our diagram, to be complete we must also consider the matter of self-discipline. I wish to thank the Rev. Roger Wagner for first calling my attention to this matter.

Self-discipline (*egkrateia*) is mentioned in Galatians 5:23 as part of the Spirit's fruit. It is only when one fails to exercise self-discipline that the process set forth in Matthew 18 comes into play. But it is also important to realize that whenever there is success reconciling parties at any subsequent stage—one-on-one, one or two others, etc.—such success is incomplete if it does not go beyond the issue of the moment to deal with the offender's problem preventively in terms of self-discipline. That is to say, the party who failed to exercise self-control also must be helped, usually by counseling, so that in the future he will be able to face similar situations without losing self-control.

The process in our diagram and the process in Matthew 18:15, when compared, look like this:

MATTHEW 18

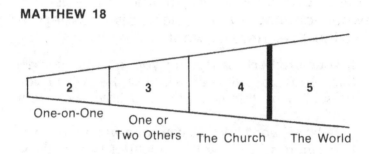

FULL PROCESS

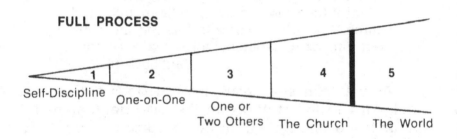

CONFIDENTIALITY

Several matters must concern us in a preliminary way. To begin with, take the ever-enlarging numbers of persons involved in the ongoing process of church discipline: first one, then two, then three or four, then the entire church, and finally the world. The implication of this biblical requirement to seek additional help in order to reclaim an offender is that Christians must never promise absolute confidentiality to any person. Frequently it is the practice of Bible-believing Christians to give assurances of absolute confidentiality, never realizing that they are following a policy that originated in the Middle Ages and that is unbiblical and contrary to Scripture (there is not a scrap of evidence in the Bible for the practice).

Both individuals and counselors must be aware of the all-important fact that absolute confidentiality prohibits the proper exercise of church discipline. If, for example, in step 2, which involves a one-on-one confrontation, one party asks the other for absolute confidentiality as a prerequisite to reconciliation, he thereby makes it impossible for the second party to move to step 3 (or beyond) in the process of church discipline, should negotiations fail at step 2. Or, when another party is called in to give counsel at stage three, if the original parties demand absolute confidentiality of this counselor they make it impossible for him to move the process to steps 4 and 5 should they be necessary. Nor could the "two or three others" function as "witnesses" as Jesus required. In other words, because absolute confidentiality is an unbiblical concept, it serves only to keep persons who need the help of others from receiving it.

Of even greater importance than the matter of hindering the process of discipline and thereby depriving those parties involved of the assistance they need, including the help of Christ working formally through His church, is the fact that absolute confidentiality requires one to make a hasty vow. No such vow to silence should ever be made. A rash vow of this sort may put us in a bind where we are obligated to God to move the process of discipline on to a larger sphere, yet our vow to silence prohibits us from doing so. We must never put ourselves in a position where we find it impossible to obey a biblical commandment because of a vow we have made. No vow must ever involve possible disobedience to God; the vow of absolute confidentiality always does.

Is it right, then, to refuse to grant any confidentiality at all? No, confidentiality is assumed in the gradual widening of the sphere of concern to other persons set forth in Matthew 18:15ff. As you read the words of our Lord in that passage, you get the impression that it is only reluctantly, when all else fails, that more and more persons may be called in. The ideal seems to be to keep the matter as narrow as possible. When Jesus speaks of step 2 (one-on-one; the first step mentioned in Matthew 18:15), He says, "Convict him of his sin privately, with just the two of you present." There is an obvious concern for confidentiality. At each stage thereafter, that concern seems equally important as other persons are brought in only when the offender refuses to listen.[1]

What then does one say when asked to keep a matter in confidence? We ought to say, "I am glad to keep confidence in the way that the Bible instructs me. That means, of course, I shall never involve others unless God requires me to do so." In other words, we must not promise *absolute* confidentiality, but rather, confidentiality that is consistent with biblical requirements. No Christian can rightly ask another for more than that. However, because of the widespread ignorance of church discipline and of the biblical position on confidentiality, it is often necessary to explain what you mean by biblical requirements in the matter and

---

[1] At each point, a refusal of one or the other parties to "listen" is the operative factor that moves the course of discipline along to the next stage. The matter, therefore, is not arbitrary, but it does require a judgment call as to when such a stage has been reached. Refusal to listen would involve an unwillingness on the part of one or both parties to continue to speak and act in ways that are calculated to bring about reconciliation. Adequate time must be given, and a sufficient number of attempts at reconciliation should be made to be certain that it is impossible to get anywhere without advancing to the next step. Except in cases of divisiveness (to be discussed *infra*), it is always wise to err, if need be, on the side of caution, giving the benefit of the doubt in love (cf. 1 Corinthians 13:7, believing and hoping the best of all involved).

sometimes even to go into detail as I have in the preceding paragraphs.

The matter of confidentiality has arisen as an issue in some pro-life centers for unwed mothers. Certain centers have opted for giving prospective mothers assurance of absolute confidentiality. But this means that when a Christian girl plans to have an abortion in spite of their counsel to the contrary, the center pledges not to tell her parents or her church. That leads not only to making an unacceptable vow, but possibly also to having complicity in the death of the child.

ALL STEPS, ALWAYS?

Obviously, there are situations in which a matter does not originate between two persons and, therefore, does not require the use of all the steps of discipline. For instance, in 1 Corinthians 5 we read about a man who was having sexual relations with his father's wife (that is, his stepmother). It was a matter of notoriety since they were living together; it was not a matter between two individuals, but a matter between the man and the church. Paul begins discipline at stage five, telling the church to "put him out of the midst." He does not go through the previous steps of discipline at all.

Was Paul exercising some special, apostolic prerogative? Absolutely not. As a matter of fact, he calls the church "arrogant" (v. 2) for not removing him on their own without his prompting.

Suppose there is a Christian woman who becomes pregnant. She is repentant. She has asked God's forgiveness. What should she do now? In a few months it will be apparent that she is an unwed mother; the matter will then be public. You should advise her to come before the elders of the church to explain her position. When the elders have ascertained that she is in fact repentant, they should forgive her in the name of Christ and His church and announce to the congregation the fact that "so-and-so has become pregnant out of wedlock, has sought and received forgiveness in repentance before God and the elders, and is to be forgiven and received by all in love."[2] Warning should be given against any gossip or other wrong attitudes, and exhortations to assist and affirm love toward her should be made. This means that you have begun and ended discipline at step 4.[3]

The case in the preceding paragraphs raises another important point. Since the matter was initiated and resolved at stage four, before the church, it is not a matter for the world. This means that any announcement of the sin and repentance should be limited to the church *alone.* Guests and visitors might be dismissed before making the announcement at a church service or, possibly, a letter might be sent to the congregation (including a warning that no one but the membership is entitled to the information in it). But whatever way it is done, the matter should be kept at stage four; the world has no part in it.

Let's take up another issue. Some think that if one Christian differs with the writings or public statements of another Christian on a point of doctrine, without rancor or any problem between them as persons, he is wrong for stating the differences publicly before going

---

[2] Although I shall have more to say about it in a future chapter, here I should at least mention the fact that a record of her repentance and the fact that the church considers the matter closed should be made in the elders' minutes to guard the future welfare of the repentant party.

[3] Of course, she may need help in matters leading to self-discipline, so that counseling also may be indicated.

privately to the brother with whom he disagrees. That is a misconception. First of all, there is no unreconciled condition between them; they simply differ. Secondly, therefore, there is no matter of church discipline involved. Thirdly, even if this were a matter of discipline, the first party spoke or wrote publicly—he put it before the church or the world; he did not speak privately. For that reason it is appropriate for the second brother to write or speak as publicly as the first did in refuting what he thinks is a wrong interpretation of the Scriptures and which, therefore, he believes may hurt the church if he doesn't. There may, of course, be doctrines so seriously wrong that he would have to prefer charges against him before whatever authorities of the church may be available for such purposes, and a disciplinary process may be set in motion at the fourth stage.[4] But not all differences of belief or interpretation call for disciplinary action.

There are times, naturally, when a Priscilla and an Aquila will find it appropriate to "take aside" a modern-day Apollos and "explain God's way to him more accurately" (Acts 18:26b), but not every situation either allows for this or demands it.

Consider another scenario in which the regular process of church discipline begins, not with step 1 or 2 but with step 3. Two Christians have a dispute that has led to bad feelings between them that do not disappear. Yet neither of them has asked for the help of one or two others. A third Christian becomes aware of the

---

[4]The process of discipline for doctrinal error is not substantially different from the discipline that Jesus discusses in Matthew 18. Again, apart from apostasy (rejecting the gospel; Hebrews 6:1–6), no one is removed from the church for other errors who willingly receives instruction, but only those who refuse it (though elders and deacons, of whom greater doctrinal precision must be expected, may be deposed from office).

problem and of the rift between the parties; he sees them "caught" in some sin from which they are not extricating themselves. So, in obedience to Galatians 6:1–2 he moves in to help "restore" them to a place of usefulness in Christ's church. Out of loving concern he temporarily bears their burdens in this altercation so that, being restored to their places in the church, they will soon be able to carry their own share of the load once again (v. 5).[5] In this case, informal discipline is instituted at its last stage. If the third party is able to help the two persons[6] to become reconciled, then the matter ceases at that point and need never take on formal dimensions.

Change the scenario just a bit. This time there is one Christian caught in sin. Another, in obedience to Galatians 6, goes to help him. Help is rejected. The second Christian continues to offer help in spite of the refusal, as indeed he should; he is rejected again, and perhaps again and again. He continues to offer help since the problem has not been solved and, as a matter of fact, has grown more serious. Finally, the one caught in sin becomes angered at the other for his persistence and no longer will talk with him about the matter. What must happen then? Clearly, a Matthew 18:15 situation has arisen out of the friendly offers of help: the two are now unreconciled. So the would-be helper approaches him once more to talk about that problem to bring about reconciliation between them.

---

[5] I have written extensively on Galatians 6:1–2 in a book entitled *Ready to Restore*, which see for details about how to do this.

[6] Strangely, some never think of using church discipline, even informal discipline, when the two parties are husband and wife. Why not? A Christian husband and wife are not merely married persons, they are also brother and sister in Christ's church. Most marital problems could be resolved early by active, informal disciplinary action.

Refusal will lead to advancing the matter as far along the discipline continuum as necessary.

So, there are any number of angles; discipline may begin at any stage in the process. Basically, the rule of thumb by which to determine where the matter should be handled is this: deal with the problem on the level at which it presents itself, making every effort to involve no one other than those already involved.

We shall have occasion to deal with some of these problems as we work our way through the five steps in the next five chapters.

4

Self-Discipline

Enkrateia, mentioned in Galations 5:23 as a part of the fruit of the Spirit, a word that is usually translated "self-control," is probably the closest term to what we call "self-discipline." The former English designation, emphasizing "control," stresses the effect, whereas the latter places the emphasis on the cause: "discipline." Discipline is the process that leads to the peaceful, orderly condition of self-control in the individual.

The Greek term has to do with curbing or restraining desire, a use that is plainly seen in the verbal form of the word in 1 Corinthians 7:9: "But if they cannot *control* themselves they must marry, since it is better to marry than to burn." Here, of course, Paul is speaking of the control of sexual desire; but neither the noun nor the verb is restricted to such a referent. While both are especially related to sexual control, they are by no means restricted to that usage even in the New Testament. For instance, in 1 Corinthians 9:25 the verbal use of the word refers to self-discipline in athletics: "And everyone who competes in a contest *exercises self-control* in all things."

The idea at the root of the word group has to do with "holding" or "gripping" something. The self-controlled person is one who has a hold or grip on himself, especially on his desires or habitual responses. That is precisely what our reference to the first step in the process of discipline is all about—persons who have such a grip on themselves that they are able to handle problems and relationships in the church and world without the need of help from others. Though there is no such thing as a "submarine Christian" (the German equivalent to our expression, "lone-wolf Christian," though of course they call him a "U-boat Christian") and though we all are interdependent on the other members of the body, the self-controlled Christian is someone who knows when to seek help himself rather than waiting for others to offer it. He is self-disciplined and, as a result, self-controlled even in that.

To be self-controlled does not do away with the strength and wisdom of the Spirit given through His Word. Indeed, *egkrateia* is said to be the fruit of the Spirit (i.e., the result of the Spirit's work) in a believer. This work of the Spirit makes him a sturdy, dependable person to whom others turn for encouragement and help. It makes him the sort of Christian who rarely gets into trouble with others because of indiscretions of word or deed, and who, if and when he does offend, quickly rectifies the situation *on his own*. That means he is sensitive to pleasing and not grieving the Spirit who has worked *egkrateia* in him in the first place, and he is ever ready to rely on the Spirit for help in the future. His self-control, then, is not a control that comes from himself but from the Spirit, and it is *self*-control only in the sense that he is not dependent on other human beings for that control.

THE BEGINNING AND THE END

In an earlier chapter I spoke of the importance of self-discipline to the process of church discipline, alluding to the fact that all discipline begins and ends with self-discipline. I now want to enlarge on that statement, explaining what I meant and drawing out an important implication that should flow from it.

Self-discipline is the beginning and end of church discipline because it is the most basic element in all discipline. It is discipline of the most mature type. Discipline begins in a child's life as discipline by others; much of the work of child training involved in *paideia* and *musar* has to do with bringing a child to maturity, that maturity consisting of his ability to discipline himself in the ways of God.

The process of child training that the Bible sets forth is one in which the control of parents is gradually replaced by the control of the Spirit through the Word as a child matures into a youth, willing and able to follow the Scriptures on his own without the continued, watchful instruction of parents. The mature person obeys not for fear of punishment or hope of reward, but out of gratitude to God who sent the Savior to die for him. He wants to please God rather than his parents, others, or even himself.

The ideal set forth in Proverbs (which is a Hebrew training manual for youth) is for a person to be able to "control his spirit" (Proverbs 16:32), "control his tongue" (Proverbs 17:27), and "control his anger" (Proverbs 19:11). The New Testament ideal is the person who walks according to the Spirit's law,[1] rather than the law

---

[1] Chrysostom, *Homily* ix, 1 Timothy 2:11–15 says, ". . . for good habits formed will be to them as a law." In this statement lies the explanation of the word *law* in the latter part of Romans 7 and the early verses of Romans 8. The law "in the members" is the regular,

of sin (Romans 8:2). Both pictures are sketches of a believer who is under the guidance and control of God Himself. The Book of Proverbs represents the work of the father and the mother as bringing the child to this place of independence by teaching biblical truth which shall follow and guide the child throughout life, long after they are gone. (See numerous statements to this effect in chapters 1–9, notably in chapter 5.)

It is this strong biblical emphasis that indicates self-discipline is at once the beginning and the end of church discipline. By that I mean, just as parents want their children to become less and less controlled by them and more and more under the control of the Spirit by means of His internalized Word, written and impressed upon their hearts (Deuteronomy 6:6, etc.), so too each of the other four stages of discipline, when successful, should result not merely in setting a matter straight, but also in helping the restored person become more self-disciplined.

Unfortunately, even where discipline is properly applied according to steps 2 through 5, frequently the

---

sinful, habitual way in which the members of the body have learned to respond. When something happens over and over again with unfailing regularity, we call it a law. That is the way in which Paul speaks of the sinful responses of his flesh (the body wrongly habituated) with which he struggled. Notice that according to Romans 7 the "law of sin" is "in his members." This law fights against the Spirit-habituated mind and must be conquered. It was because he "presented" the members of his body to sin as his master (Romans 6:12–13, 19) that this fleshly body became wrongly habituated to sin and these bodily responses became a law. Now he must present the members of the body to God for righteous purposes (6:19b; 12:1). As the body of sin (dominated and used by sin) developed its laws, or regular ways of responding to life, so too the body now led by the Spirit may develop a new law (a regular, habitual righteous lifestyle). According to Romans 8:2, this new law of the Spirit sets one free from the old ways and replaces them with His new ones.

need for helping the repentant offender to become self-disciplined is not recognized. God insists that the restored offender be "assisted" (that is the basic idea of *parakaleo*) as he is reassimilated into the body after being put out of the body (2 Corinthians 2:7). A significant part of such assistance by the church in formal discipline (stages 4 and 5) must be teaching himself discipline in the area of his offense. A forgiven adulterer needs more than restoration; the thought life and daily habits that contributed to the act, as well as his bad relationship with his wife, must be dealt with. The party or parties informally involved in helping someone at stages 2 and 3 should offer or suggest counseling aimed at achieving the same goal. Apart from this additional help, the brother or sister will more than likely fall into the same sort of difficulty again.

It is not possible here to go into the details of helping another to achieve self-discipline. I have discussed the subject at some length in two books in particular: *Godliness Through Discipline* (Presbyterian and Reformed Publishing Co., 1972) and *Ready to Restore* (Presbyterian and Reformed Publishing Co., 1981).

For now, let me simply note the importance of this ancillary factor, which, though not in itself a part of remedial church discipline, could be the most valuable outcome of it. What better time is there to stress the importance of self-discipline in an area of one's life than when that person is repentant over some incident that has led to the application of discipline?[2] True

---

[2] One of the benefits of church discipline is its tendency to dislodge stubborn or careless Christians from sin in which they have become entrenched. Often, for the first time, discipline makes counseling fruitful. Indeed, even the threat of discipline can have this beneficial effect in some instances. In many cases where persons have despaired of ever seeing movement or change in

repentance is essentially a desire to think, be, and do differently. In most cases where discipline is necessary, the offense grows out of a pattern of life and is not a first or one-time event. It is in freeing oneself from such lifestyles that the person especially needs help.

Stage 1, self-discipline, warrants an entire book in itself. Perhaps someday such a book will be forthcoming. But now we must move on to step 2.

---

another, they have forgotten (or overlooked) the possibilities for change that may be opened up by the proper application (or threat) of church discipline. I have used the word *threat* twice, not to indicate that church discipline is ordinarily a dangerous or fearful thing; indeed, it is truly a blessing and a privilege. Rather, I have used the word to indicate how it is often *perceived* by others.

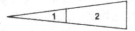

5

One-on-One

With step 2 we begin to consider the ways in which one Christian seeks to help another through the use of discipline. In self-discipline, no one else is involved; the believer deals with his sin alone before God. If, for example, he has sinful thoughts relating to another person, he does not disclose them to that person; he handles them in confession and repentance before God alone. The principle followed in Matthew 18:15ff. is that a matter must be kept as narrow as the event itself. In the case of self-discipline, the only parties to the event are the believer and God. That principle applies at the beginning and is operative throughout.

Now we turn to the first of those stages of church discipline in which others participate. It is the stage where one believer confronts another about what he believes to be the other's sin.

The presence of others can certainly complicate the situation. The successful use of discipline by others, whether it be by one or many, presupposes the knowledge of a number of principles and practices relating to the intricacies in the interrelationships that develop in the process of discipline. Apart from such knowledge, the participating believer may fail to act as he should and, in the end, may do harm rather than good.

I do not say this to discourage the use of church discipline, nor to make anyone hesitate in following the steps of discipline as outlined by Christ; indeed, the very opposite is my concern. Yet, because of the vast ignorance of the facts of church discipline and because of the many erroneous ideas bandied about concerning it, pastors and church leaders should regularly instruct their congregations in the full range of its principles and practices. This would work to help avoid needless injury. Anyone reading and following the biblical teachings in this book ought to be able to wend his way successfully through the intricacies of church discipline with little or no confusion.

INFORMAL DISCIPLINE

Looking back at the full diagram in chapter 3 (page 27), you will notice that I have called steps 1 through 3 "informal discipline" and steps 4 and 5 "formal discipline." What I am getting at here is the fact that the church as an institution becomes involved in the process only after the first three steps have failed.

In most instances, therefore, discipline never reaches the formal stage. This is quite contrary to the ordinary concept of discipline as it is popularly held. The words "church discipline" usually suggest to people's minds that the church is officially taking action to remove someone. That is not the way that effective, regularly occurring discipline works; ordinarily, in a church that is comfortable with it, discipline achieves its objectives at stage 2 or 3. So often when someone is put out of the church for failure to repent of open, public sin, it is because there was a failure to exercise informal discipline at an earlier point before the sinful act became a habitual practice that had to be met with formal discipline.

Because informal discipline is so important, I shall take the time to investigate it in detail, especially at this second stage, where another individual first enters the picture. Let me put before you what Jesus says about stage 2:

> If your brother sins against you, go and convict him of his sin privately, with just the two of you present. If he listens to you, you have won your brother (Matthew 18:15).

THE MEANING

In this verse Jesus sketches a scenario in which one Christian ("your brother") has wronged another. In such a situation He (1) commands (2) the offended brother to (3) "go" and (4) speak with the brother (5) privately in such as way as (6) to convict him of his sin. If the brother listens (i.e., if he confesses his sin and seeks forgiveness), reconciliation takes place.

In this summary I have numbered the essential elements involved in step 2. The first is that Jesus leaves no options whenever sin separates brothers; He *commands* informal discipline to bring about reconciliation. He does not say that it would be *nice* if the offended party were to go and seek reconciliation; He requires him to do so. Whenever an unreconciled condition exists between two believers, there is no option left: discipline must be pursued.

All the reservations, objections, and hesitations that people have about discipline are irrelevant. Jesus does not leave the matter up to us; He *tells* us what to do. If there are problems about pursuing informal discipline, He expects you to solve them; He does not allow them to short-circuit the process. If you are ignorant of the ways and means of carrying on church discipline, He holds you responsible for learning what you do not already know. Jesus does not suggest, He *requires* the use of informal discipline.

GOING TO THE OFFENDER

The next two elements in the process (3, 4) direct the offended brother to go to the offender. It is true that in Matthew 5:23–24, Jesus requires the offender to go immediately to any brother whom he may have offended and be reconciled to him—even leaving his gift at the altar. (Jesus pictures him as interrupting an act of worship to do so, thereby showing the high priority He places on good relations between Christians; cf. 1 Peter 3:7.) It is also true, however (just as it is also in Luke 17:3), that the offended party has the very same obligation. When discord between believers takes place, ideally they ought to meet each other on the way to one another's house to seek reconciliation.

But why should the offended party be required to go? He may protest, "I haven't done anything; why should I have to go? Let him come to me!" But according to Christ, that will not do. Why not? Because the offender may enlarge the offense by not going (i.e., not obeying the command in Matthew 5:23–24), or he may not realize that his brother has taken offense. Let me speak to this latter matter for a moment.

Mary has not seen Jane for some time since Jane

has been out of town on a vacation. Now Jane has returned. Mary spots her in church and determines to say hello after the service. After the benediction, Mary hurries to the other side of the church to where Jane has been sitting. By now Jane is on her way out of the church. Mary calls to her, "Hello, Jane. Wait for me!" But Jane sticks her nose up in the air and sails out of the church as quickly as she can, without so much as a "Howdy do" to Mary.

Mary can respond in one of two ways. If she does what many Christians do, she will say, "Hmmph! Well! If that's the way she wants to act, then let her go! She can come to me the next time; that will be the last time I go after her!" And so a friendship is ruined, the work of Christ is hindered as the body is weakened, and the honor of God is compromised.

But if Mary understands church discipline and is willing to obey Christ, she will not settle for that. Instead, she will follow Jane from the church and search her out. Suppose that she has done so. She says, "Jane! What's wrong? I was so glad to see you that I hurried over to your aisle and called to you but you stuck your nose in the air and left the church, ignoring me, as if I didn't exist. What's wrong? I must tell you that I was greatly hurt."

In this little fictional episode Jane responds, "Oh, Mary! I'm so sorry! I didn't have the faintest idea what was happening. Let me explain. I was sitting through church thinking about only one thing. I have a bad cold and my nose began to run. But I left my handkerchief here in the car. I was afraid that since the preacher preached so long I'd drip all over my new dress and my Bible, so as soon as the benediction was over, oblivious to everything else, I put my head back so I wouldn't drip and rushed for the car." After a good laugh and a hug or two Mary and Jane are reconciled. Indeed, there was no offense at all—only a misunderstanding.

What a silly scenario! you say. I agree. But I have counseled persons who were separated from each other for more than twenty years by some misunderstanding that was every bit as silly. You see, only the offended person knows that there is a problem when there has been a misunderstanding. It is his toes that have been stepped on—accidentally or not at all in some cases—so that, even if his brother isn't, he is always aware of the supposed offense. That is another reason why the offended is required to go. If he were allowed not to go, many cases would never be dealt with. But Jesus wants no loose ends; He wants every personal difficulty between brothers resolved. The brother with the sore toes must go because he is always the one who is aware.

WHAT TO SAY

When a brother or sister goes to a supposed offender, he or she is to speak to him so as to convict him (4, 6). However, Luke 17:3 adds a dimension to this matter. According to Christ's words there, the offended brother does not convict the offender initially, making charges and calling for repentance. Rather, he must first go to the offender and rebuke him *in a tentative manner.* (The word in Luke 17:3 is not *elengcho,* "convict," which is the term used in Matthew 18:15ff., a less detailed passage, but *epitimao,* which means "to rebuke tentatively.") That is to say, he first goes and explains the situation as he has perceived or experienced it, saying something like this: "As far as I can see, you have wronged me in such and such a way, but if you have an explanation, I am ready to hear it before passing final judgment."

This tentative rebuke allows for explanation. As in the case of Mary and Jane, there is opportunity to clear up any misunderstanding. And even if there was a real offense, it might have been quite unintentional (e.g., splashing mud on a friend without realizing that your car even went through a mud puddle). The tentative rebuke allows for the statement and discussion of the facts and the working out of the solution to any problems that may have arisen over the incident.

Moreover, even when there has been an offense that was intentional, the tentative rebuke provides a fitting prelude to conviction. The attitude of the one offended is restrained thereby, and this may more likely lead to a quick and easier reconciliation than if he had come charging up with his accusations, making no allowances for explanations at all.

But where an offense has been given, nothing short of conviction will do. The conviction of which Jesus spoke is not the subjective feeling that the word is used to indicate in Christian circles today, but the effective use of objective evidence to convict a person of the crime of which he has been accused: the word comes from the law courts. That is why I have used the language I have in the previous sentence; it expresses exactly what the word means. Therefore, the Lord does not require you to bring another to feelings of guilt and sorrow as the modern usage would seem to indicate. Rather, you are to compile your case so that you are successful in proving the offense has occurred.

The distinction that I have just made is important. Among other things, it implies that if you do not have a good case, with facts to back up any accusation you make, you should not take offense in the first place. Too many Christians become angered, hurt, or otherwise upset on quite insufficient grounds. They make accusations recklessly. They act on suppositions.

That in itself is unchristian and, incidentally, in some instances a reason for instituting church discipline against the accuser, because it is an unloving act spawned by an unloving attitude. In 1 Corinthians 13:7 Paul says that love "believes all things, hopes all things." If those words mean anything, at the very least they indicate that the loving attitude and action is to give the brother the benefit of the doubt in every case where it is possible. When there is the slightest doubt, you must interpret an action by your brother in the most charitable way.

PRIVACY

The last element (6) is privacy. When the offense is between two persons, and between them alone, no others should be brought into the picture if it is possible to bring about reconciliation without them. Before, during, and after the period when the second step is in force, the issue should not be mentioned to anyone else if reconciliation takes place. As in every step before and after, the discussion is to be kept as narrow as the offense.

However, as we have seen in a previous chapter, this does not mean that a promise of absolute confidentiality should be given. It may be that reconciliation cannot be effected in step 2; in that case it would be necessary to involve others if Christ's command is to be obeyed. So one must not bind himself to secrecy by a rash vow that would keep him from obeying Christ. Rather, he should promise to keep the matter quiet *at this stage* in the proceedings, bringing no one else in on it, in accordance with the expressed requirements of Christ. Jesus does insist, however, that no one else should be informed of what is happening as long as the matter remains at this level.

RECONCILIATION

"You have won your brother." That is what Jesus says. To win him is to become reconciled to him (cf. Matthew 5:24). The word for reconciliation is *diallasso*, which means "to exchange enmity for friendship." What does reconciliation involve?

Jesus does not say that the sinning brother is to "apologize." It is disappointing to see in Christian books everywhere—even in books dealing with the matter of church discipline—authors settling for this unbiblical and totally inadequate invention that the world substitutes for forgiveness. Apologizing and forgiving are two different things.

Because I have treated this matter at length elsewhere, I shall but mention it here. Saying "I'm sorry" only tells another how you feel; it asks him to do nothing about the offense. When you say, "I sinned against God and He has forgiven me; now I want to confess that I have also sinned against you; will you forgive me too?" you ask for a decision on his part. When apologizing, you keep the ball in your own court; when you seek forgiveness, you toss the ball to the other party. He must now do something with it.

When he says, "I forgive you," he makes a promise (which is what forgiveness is) never to raise the matter again. He promises not to bring it up to you, nor to anyone else, and not to sit and brood on it. The matter, he assures you, is closed. A promise can be made whether one feels like it or not; and it can be kept whether one feels like it or not.

But because forgiveness is the promise not to bring up a matter again, it is granted only on repentance (the other's word is sufficient; cf. Luke 17:4). While you must forgive in your heart and not carry bitterness against another, you may not *grant* him forgiveness (i.e., promise not to bring up the matter again) until he repents. Otherwise, you could not carry the matter on through the other steps of discipline were it necessary to do so.

Reconciliation is a matter of restoring friendship, so it is not enough merely to bury a matter; both parties must work toward a new and proper relationship for the future. Forgiveness simply clears the way for the friendship that grows out of true reconciliation. This means effort, time, and whatever else may be required to bring it about should be given to assure that the weld becomes stronger than it was before the break. Only in that way will it become manifest that "where sin abounded, grace far more abounded" (Romans 5:20).

Often, because the full intent of reconciliation— restoration of Christian friendship—is missed, forgiveness merely closes an issue but does nothing about the future relationship of the parties involved. When no efforts are made to restore and build a better relationship than ever before, the relationship usually deteriorates in spite of forgiveness. That is because the focus has been on getting one to admit he is wrong (or, on the other hand, on getting someone off one's back) instead of focusing on the restoration of relationship.

EVERY LITTLE THING?

Sometimes the question is raised, Do I have to go to my brother about every little offense? The answer is *no*. Love covers a multitude of sins (Proverbs 10:12). To cover sins, or to "overlook an offense" (Proverbs 19:11b), is a glorious thing. If we had to bring up every rub between us we'd probably spend all our time doing so. No, any offense that doesn't get between us and the one who committed it—does not need to be raised. But anything that creates an unreconciled state between us and another must be brought up and dealt with. That is to say, any matter which is carried over to another day, any matter which makes you feel different toward that person for more than a passing moment, any matter that throws love's covers off must be brought up.

Of course, if the sin which your brother commits against you is debilitating to him and he is not dealing with it adequately in his own life, you may well have to raise the matter anyway, on the basis of Galatians 6:1–2, even if you yourself could overlook the matter. In that case you will raise it for his sake. Both in overlooking or in bringing up matters for the sake of another, it is important to be very sure of your motives; these are areas in which you may easily deceive yourself.

So, step 2. Most instances will be settled at this level without going higher. More of this sort of activity should take place in the church. On the other hand, there are some few—very few—people who take advantage of the discipline process and spend an inordinate amount of time confronting others. Such persons should be taught the glory of overlooking an offense and the art of covering sins in love. If they refuse to learn, they themselves may become divisive and may need to be confronted by others.

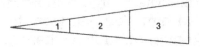

6

One or Two Others

How often should an offended person go to another before moving on to step 3 in the disciplinary process? Is it a matter of the length of time, or the number of times? Neither. In Matthew 18:16 the operative phrase is "if he won't listen to you." At each stage what moves the process ahead a step is the refusal of the offender to be reconciled: "and if he refuses to listen to them" (v. 17); "and if he refuses to listen to the church" (v. 17). One moves on to the next step in church discipline only when progress is not being made toward reconciliation because the other person has dug in his heels and is unwilling to do whatever is necessary to be reconciled.

This does not imply that you have been to him but once and, upon his refusal to listen, you then move on. No. The refusal must be a genuine one. This means that if, in the heat of the battle, he will not listen to reason, you will wait until he has had time to cool off and then try again. Perhaps you will find it necessary to try several times before stepping up the process. You may wish to vary your approach. You will want to be sure that you have gone in a spirit of meekness and that you have not alienated him by the manner in which you approached him. You will want to look for signs that he is weakening and follow these, if possible, to a successful outcome.

Moreover, you must distinguish carefully between unwillingness to listen and a failure to understand or to accept your viewpoint on the matter. If the brother or sister continues to discuss the matter with you, asking for further evidence, saying that he understands the facts differently, etc., or if he believes that your interpretation of biblical verses that bear upon the case is wrong, surely you are obligated to consider these matters.

As long as a reasonable discussion of these questions continues, you cannot charge him with failure to listen. But if the discussion ceases—if there is a failure to deal with issues in what you think is the biblical way and he tells you, in effect, "Look, we've said all there is to say on this matter. You are wrong and that is it"—you then have grounds for moving ahead. But you must first be sure that you have been willing to listen to him as well.

So it is neither the length of time any step may take nor the number of times reconciliation attempts are made that determines when to move to a further stage; rather, it is the willingness or unwillingness of the party or parties involved to continue negotiations.

The operative phrase in Matthew 18:16, as we have seen, is "if he won't listen to you." In verse 17 the wording is stronger: "If he refuses to listen. . . ." The term *parakouo,* used twice in verse 17, which I have translated "if he refuses to listen," occurs elsewhere in the New Testament only in Mark 5:36, where it may have the meaning of "not paying attention to." It describes a refusal to listen that amounts to ignoring the seriousness of a confrontation or its content. It indicates that the party who refuses has determined to go his own way and "will not heed" or simply "ignores" the words of others.

In the case of refusal at stages 3 and 4, therefore, reasoned and biblical advice from disinterested parties is rejected and the party insists on his own interpretations, inclinations, and desires. In Matthew 18:16, where the offender "won't hear," though this is plainly wrong, it is more understandable; there is an emotional block between the parties. But in these later stages of discipline, where no such obstacle imposes itself, ignoring advice and help indicates a more stubborn willfulness. This very attitude left unchecked is what in the long run leads to one's removal from the organized church.

WITNESSES ONLY?

I believe that J. Carl Laney is clearly wrong when he sees the witnesses mentioned in Matthew 18:16 as witnesses to the offense committed.[1] Jesus said:

> But if he won't listen to you, take with you one or two others so that by the mouth of two or three witnesses every word may be confirmed. And if he refuses to listen to them, tell it to the church (vv. 16–17a).

There are several reasons why Laney's interpretation is wrong. If witnesses to the offense (Laney's view) are brought into the picture only after a private conference is held, then that matter was not private to begin

[1] J. Carl Laney, *A Guide to Church Discipline* (Minneapolis: Bethany House, 1985), pp. 53–54.

with—there were witnesses. The very idea of keeping the matter private between the only two who know about it is vitiated. Moreover, the sequence of reluctantly opening the matter up to more and more persons (vv. 15–17) is radically disturbed. Of greatest significance, however, is that the wording of the text does not support that view. Let's see why not.

The "witnesses" are not *merely* witnesses. They are first counselors who seek to reunite the two estranged parties. That is indicated in the words "if he refuses to listen to them." They are pictured as actively participating in the reconciliation process. It is when the refusal takes place, and only then, that they turn into witnesses. They do not appear as witnesses in this informal stage (to whom would they witness?); they will become witnesses if and when the matter is formally brought before the church. Paul makes it clear that issues may not be entertained by the church unless witnesses are present (2 Corinthians 13:1).

What the witnesses attest to and confirm is "every word." That is to say, they are able to witness to the words that were spoken by themselves, to the words of the brother trying to bring about reconciliation, and to the words of refusal by the one who stubbornly ignored them. They do not witness to "events," which would include actions as well as words, but to *words* only. Many cases of estrangement occur because of acts as well as words. But Jesus describes them as witnesses who report words alone. Moreover, in the first instance they are not called "witnesses" but "one or two others." They turn into witnesses only upon the refusal of one or more of the parties to repent and be reconciled. They witness to the discussions that occur during step 3, not about the sin that occasioned step 2.

Who should these counselor/witnesses be? Jesus does not specify any more particularly than to say "one or two others." This means that any two Christians may be called upon to help. However, since these persons must offer counsel and possibly will become witnesses if that counsel is spurned, it would be wise, where available, to call on persons who are best able to offer wise counsel and whose words of testimony, if needed, would be respected by the congregation. Elders, deacons, and even pastors would be prime persons to select, as long as it is clear that at stage 3 they appear only as private Christians and not in their official character.[2] Sometimes under the circumstances, this is hard to do, so it is often wise to ask capable leaders in the church who do not bear office to serve. If persons highly respected by both of the estranged parties can be found, it would seem good to tap them.

Asking someone to serve as a counselor/witness must also be done properly. To assure privacy, the name of the offender should not be revealed to a potential counselor/witness until he has agreed to participate. It is the duty of any Christian who is asked, to serve, and only for the gravest reasons should he refuse (see Galatians 6:1–2).

WHAT THE COUNSELOR/WITNESSES DO

It would seem that something like the following would be an appropriate way for these counselor/witnesses to approach their task:

1. They would make an appointment to go, together with the person who appealed to them, to see the one who allegedly refused to listen. They would be

---

[2] In such cases, care must be taken to be sure all parties understand that the presence of a church officer does not mean that step 4—official, formal discipline—has been initiated.

very careful, as all counselors should, not to prejudice the case by allowing the brother who enlisted them to fill their minds with all sorts of negative "facts" about the offense or about previous attempts to bring about reconciliation that failed. Beyond the bare facts that such a situation exists, they should refuse to accept any other negative material until the supposed offender is present.

Otherwise they will run the danger of gossip, slander, and "talking down a brother behind his back" (*katalaleo*), which James forbids (James 4:11). And because they were enlisted by the opposite party, the supposed offender will tend to think that they have "ganged up" on him. They should probably tell him, upon making the appointment, that they have not allowed any negative discussion concerning him to be carried on and that they are coming completely open to hearing both sides in accordance with Proverbs 18:17.

2. If the brother refuses to agree to an appointment, or does not keep it, they should do all they can to persuade him to do so. They may call several times, and if necessary, they may even show up on his doorstep without announcement. When all has failed, they should warn him that they will have to carry testimony of his refusal and the words that he has spoken back to the church when his offended brother institutes formal discipline. They should inform him of the serious nature of his willfulness, that he is on dangerous ground, and that persistence in his refusal to hear could lead to removal from Christ's church.

3. If the offending party is willing to meet with them and the brother who enlisted them, they should take charge, designating one of the two (if that many is chosen) to be the leader of the discussion (though all

would participate). They would ask both parties to bring their evidence and try to gather all the pertinent facts.

They should probably begin with the accuser and hear his story about the offense and his subsequent unsuccessful attempts to bring about reconciliation. They should ascertain from him a clear statement that, in pursuing discipline, his desire is to bring about a restoration of fellowship and friendship. They may want to question him on various points and advise him about unsubstantiated accusations if there are any.

Finally, they should indicate whether in their opinion the accuser has a convincing case. If they think otherwise, they may wish to urge him to drop the accusation, lovingly give the benefit of the doubt to his brother, and restore fellowship. At times they may even find it necessary to call on him to seek forgiveness from the accused for lack of love in accepting rumor or false evidence or in making accusations that he cannot corroborate with evidence.

4. If they think that the accuser has a prima facie case, they should move on to hear the explanation or defense by the accused. They should be careful to extract all facts relevant to the issue even if the data are not immediately forthcoming. As they listen, they should be alert not only to facts, but also to attitudes on the part of both parties. At times they may find it necessary to calm them down or to rebuke one or the other for intemperate language. There may even be instances in which they will find it necessary to ask one to seek the forgiveness of the other for the way in which he is carrying on the discussion.

5. If the counselors discover that an offense was in fact committed and believe that there is no mere misunderstanding (often both exist, in which case they

will endeavor to clear up misunderstandings as quickly as possible and concentrate on substantive issues), they should proceed to ascertain all the facts, evaluate these according to biblical standards, state the issues in biblical terms, and suggest a plan for solving the problem based on biblical principles. (In dealing with such problems, all the principles of reconciliation in counseling articulated in many places in my other books will come into play.)

If they are successful in reaching a God-honoring solution to the problem (i.e., one that conforms to Scripture, not one that compromises biblical principles), they will want to set up future appointments for the two to work on reestablishing a proper, growing relationship. When reconciliation is the goal, they will not settle for forgiveness alone (see the previous chapter for more on this subject).

6. If one or the other parties is dissatisfied with the proposed solution, or one or the other refuses to agree to the restoration of fellowship, the counselors should make every attempt to get them to do so, hearing all they have to say and working hard to bring about the desired biblical result. But if, after all attempts have been made—including as many conferences as necessary—no reconciliation seems possible, they shall warn the recalcitrant brother as stated in point 2 and advise the other brother to refer the matter to the whole church. If for some reason he should refuse to do so, they themselves would be obligated to do it (Galatians 6:1-2). They cannot stand by, knowing the situation and knowing that all the resources of Christ have not been exhausted. They must make the further attempt to bring about restoration.

An entire book could be written at this point, detailing what and what not to do under various circumstances. That is impossible and inappropriate now. I can only direct you for further help to the numerous works on biblical counseling that are available. However, some matters applicable to counseling at this stage—for instance, when the parties involved are from different congregations and different denominations—will be treated in a later chapter.

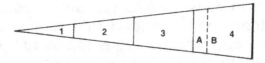

7

Tell It to the Church

We leave the realm of informal discipline as we move from step 3 to step 4 in the disciplinary process. This is a major change. It means that the church officially now takes cognizance of the problem. It also means that the seriousness of the problem has progressed to the point where it has reached the court of last resort. A brother under official discipline is in a danger zone and should be told so. Step 4 is the last opportunity for the willful brother or sister to repent and be reconciled under the loving care of members of the church.

Of course, a matter may not have progressed to this point through all the preceding steps of discipline; it is possible, as in the case of incest mentioned in 1 Corinthians 5, for a matter to *originate* at the official, formal level. When an offense against an individual or the church is so open and apparent to all that it is a matter of public fame (in 1 Corinthians 5:1 Paul puts it this way: "It is *generally* reported ...."), then the officers of the church may begin disciplinary action at step 4 without going through the previous steps. Indeed, if they do not do so, they are remiss, as Paul indicates in verse 2: "And you are arrogant! Shouldn't you rather have mourned and removed from your midst the one who has done this thing?" Presumably, according to verse 6, they were "boasting" about their open-mindedness in allowing this matter to continue without discipline.

In some ways it seems that what Paul said to the church was more severe than what he said about the incestuous son. His strong reprimand of the church for failing to exercise discipline and for having a lax attitude toward sin in their midst ought to be a trenchant warning to many churches today.

TELLING THE CHURCH

Jesus' words in Matthew 18:17a are as follows:

And if he refuses to listen to them (the counselor/witnesses), tell it to the church.

Obviously, these brief words lack a clear statement about how to carry out Jesus' instructions; no process for telling the church is even outlined, let alone detailed. Therefore we shall have to piece together the ways and means as best we are able from other passages of Scripture and from an application of the principles of decency and good order that are required by God in 1 Corinthians 14.

I think it goes without saying that to tell it to the church is not to be done by a brother standing up in the middle of a worship service (in which there is a mixture of believers and unbelievers: according to 1 Corinthians 14:23–25, unconverted persons were allowed to attend Christian worship services) and declaring what has happened. That would violate the principles of good order set forth in 1 Corinthians 14, and it would also violate the command to tell it to the *church*. At this point, the world has no right to know about the matter. That fact will be elucidated later in this chapter. The church alone must hear.

These considerations mean that one must tell the church either at a closed meeting of its membership (those who are baptized and are thereby under its care and discipline), duly called by the elders in a decent and orderly manner for that purpose, or one does so by telling the elders in their capacity as representatives of the church. Frequently in the Old Testament when God wished to speak to Israel as a whole, He summoned and addressed the elders, who then conveyed His message to the people (cf. Exodus 3:15–16; 19:3, 7; Deuteronomy 31:28, 30 [here the "assembly of Israel" is clearly equated with the "assembly" of elders], etc.). This is probably the meaning of "tell it to the church": tell it to the church by telling it to the elders of the new Israel.

When the elders tell the church, they must be sure that only the members are informed of the situation. This could be done at a closed meeting of the congregation or it could be done by letter, telling each member to read and destroy the letter when he has finished reading it so that it may never fall into the hands of nonmembers. In any letter or meeting informing the congregation that a brother has refused to deal with his sin and be reconciled, clear instructions must be given not only about how to treat him while under discipline (see *infra*), but about the fact that this is privileged information, belonging to the members of the congregation alone.

THE ELDERS' PART

There is some indication that the elders themselves, being the first informed about the recalcitrant brother or sister, should seek to persuade him or her about the sin before telling the congregation at large. That is why on the diagram I have divided the fourth step into two phases (A and B) by a broken line. It is one step, in two phases, carried out decently and in order: (A) The elders officially deal with him and (B) then, if that is unsuccessful, the entire congregation does so. Now, what is the basis for such a division?

First, the idea of such a division might be indicated by the rules for good order that I have been stating. There are intricate measures to be taken carefully, and it is important at every point in the process that the elders should be in charge, guiding and taking care that nothing goes wrong. The members will need instruction. One can see this from the very nature of the case.

But there is more. There is an indication that the leadership first attempts to help the offender before turning him over to the entire congregation for admonishing. Listen to these words of Paul: "Now whoever doesn't obey what *we* (not Paul as an apostle, but as a fellow elder with others[1]) say in this letter, mark that person ..." (2 Thessalonians 3:14a). Here the congregation gets involved *after* Paul and the others who worked with him had made an effort to reach a sinning brother. And along with that order—elders, then congregation—comes instruction for the congregation as I indicated before (cf. also vv. 14–15).

---

[1] Acts 15:6 shows how the apostles worked with elders. Cf. also 1 Peter 5:1, where Peter calls himself a "fellow elder." Sometimes apostles functioned with apostolic authority; sometimes they functioned as elders only.

It would seem that there is no other adequate way to implement Christ's command while at the same time safeguarding His requirements for privacy and the good order and decency of the church.

HOW DOES IT WORK?

There are many questions and many problems associated with this fourth step of church discipline. I shall try to deal with some of them and I shall set forth a plan that approximates the biblical process as closely as possible.

When the elders tell the congregation about a disciplinary case, they do so for a reason. The ever-widening lines in our diagram indicate that the number of persons who know about the problem increases with each step, thus bringing more and more persons into the arena of help. If a brother will not discipline himself, then another must take that task on himself. If the former won't listen to the latter, then one or two others join in offering help. If the offender refuses to heed them, the church is officially informed and the elders (and, if necessary, all the the members of the congregation) confront him in a concerted attempt to bring about reconciliation and restoration.

If all this fails, he is removed from the midst of the church, and Satan and the world are providentially utilized by God to bring about repentance. (Of course, in the case of an unregenerate person such repentance will not be forthcoming unless he is subsequently regenerated.) Thus, in Christ's plan for discipline an ever-increasing number of persons become involved in the helping process.

The reason why the congregation is told is so that as a whole they may have an opportunity to help the offending, willful brother or sister come to repentance.

What should the congregation be told about their duties to the brother who is undergoing official church discipline? Basically, in the Scriptures they are told three things:

1. That brother or sister so-and-so is under discipline for a particular problem. This is essential if they are to obey Paul's command to "mark" the person (2 Thessalonians 3:14). The word used for "marking" is the word that means "to make or put a sign on him." Paul is not suggesting that we pin a scarlet letter on the offender, but he certainly does mean "*identify* him to the entire congregation." Apart from making this clear identification of the offender, the congregation could fulfill very few of their obligations to him. They could pray for an unknown offender, but they could not avoid fellowship and counsel with him.

The congregation does not need to be told the details of the offense, but it would seem that they must be told the nature of the problem if they are to confront and seek to counsel him in any meaningful way. Paul mentions the offense in 2 Thessalonians. The rule here is to say as little as necessary, but enough to enable the body to do its job. An example may be: "John is under discipline for failing to repent of his insistence that his wife should obtain an abortion."[2]

---

[2] It is clear that persons are not disciplined, moved to the next step, or removed from the church because of particular sins, as Laney seems to think. (Laney is ambiguous about this important point; see his *Guide to Church Discipline*, pp. 45, 154–55.) They are disciplined for their inability and/or unwillingness to give up those sins. They may repent at any time and remain members of the body without ever being removed from it or their cases being carried to a higher level. It is always refusal to listen—a contumacious attitude—that moves a case forward, even in the last instance, when removal is the sole remaining alternative. *Any* sin

2. The congregation may no longer fellowship with him as though nothing were wrong. They are told, "Don't mix, or mingle, with him" (2 Thessalonians 3:14; 1 Corinthians 5:9, 11), "withdraw from him" (2 Thessalonians 3:6; the word translated "withdraw," means "stand aloof; keep away from"), and "don't eat" with him (1 Corinthians 5:11). All these commands (they are not good advice, but commands) say one and the same thing: the congregation must regard the so-called brother (1 Corinthians 5:11) "as a brother" (2 Thessalonians 3:15), but as one whose status is in question. (There is some doubt about whether he is really a brother,[3] because he fails to heed the admonition of the brethren and the authority of Christ exercised by His officers in the church; by the time the entire congregation begins its task, he has gone very far in his willful disobedience and contumacy.)

But what does withdrawal mean? It means that if John calls Bill and suggests that they play a round of golf on Monday, Bill will reply by saying something like this: "John, there's nothing I'd rather do. But there is a problem. You are under the discipline of the church and have not repented. I would be happy to spend that time with you on Monday talking about the problem instead."[4] Martha asks Jill to go shopping with her. Her reply is the same. "Not to eat" means two things: (1) that normal fellowship is broken. Eating with another, in biblical times, was the sign of fellow-

---

may occasion church discipline when it is not being dealt with by the offender.

[3] This doubt is indicated by the words "so-called brother."

[4] Some wonder why one member's sin is of concern to others. All are members of Christ's body. When there is something wrong with the toe, that affects the entire body; the whole body is weakened by the sin of one member. The other members must do all possible to heal the ailing member or it will have to be amputated (step 5).

ship; (2) that the offender is forbidden to partake of the Lord's Supper because, according to 1 Corinthians 10:16–17, partaking is "communion" or fellowship, the very thing prohibited at stage 4.

This refusal of fellowship, leading to expulsion from the Lord's Supper, is the point at which "excommunication" actually takes place. That is the literal meaning of the word. Nowhere in the Bible is excommunication (removal from the fellowship of the Lord's Table) equated with what happens in step 5; rather, step 5 is called "removing from the midst, handing over to Satan," and the like. But forbidding one to eat of the Lord's Table takes place already in step 4. No more important violation of the command not to mingle and not to eat with the offender could be imagined than to partake of the Lord's Supper with him. If he refuses to heed the officers and their admonitions, Paul says that he must be removed from table fellowship and all other forms of normal fellowship in order to "shame" him into repentance (2 Thessalonians 3:14).

3. They must "counsel" him (2 Thessalonians 3:15; Galatians 6:1–2). Laney's book, having been, as I believe, wrong or confusing in many places, goes completely astray at stage 4. Laney advocates allowing the offender to partake of the Lord's Table (p. 157), agrees with a pastor who "suggests that the names of offenders ought not be brought before the church" (p. 54), confuses "excommunication" with "removing from the midst" (pp. 55–56), and applies 1 Corinthians 5 and 2 Thessalonians 3 to stage 5 rather than to stage 4 of the disciplinary process. I must also confess to confusing "excommunication" with "removal from the midst" in previous writing; I now see that this is in error and have corrected it in this volume

(see more on this in the next chapter). The other three errors are far more serious and, if followed, would totally defeat effective discipline at this stage in the process.

Discipline is not easy to do correctly or even to do at all. It involves courage and fortitude. It requires care and precision. It must be done in neither a sloppy nor a careless manner. Therefore the process must be carried on with the knowledge and assurance that what is being done is right in God's sight. But even though discipline is difficult and runs many risks, churches dare not run the greater risk of withholding a privilege and blessing provided by Christ, thus depriving sinning members of all the help He has provided for them. Nor dare they disobey Him in refusing to follow His program for church discipline lest, in the end, they find themselves disciplined by Him (cf. 1 Corinthians 11:31–32).

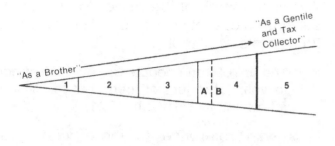

8

Removal From the Midst

When we crossed the boundary between informal and formal discipline as we moved from step 3 to step 4, we crossed a great divide that separates very treacherous from even more dangerous territory. As we now proceed from step 4 to step 5, the final step of church discipline, we take an even greater leap. All steps prior to the present one were taken within the kingdom of God; now we move from the kingdom of light into the kingdom of darkness.

On this issue, a comment can be anticipated: "I can see how removing one from the church is a purifying measure that preserves the church and brings honor to God by refusing to allow sin to permeate the ranks and exist under the auspices of His name. But I don't see how putting someone out of the church is a restorative, remedial one."

In some cases, it is not. There are tares within the church; Jesus Himself told us that. There is no way by which we can separate all the wheat from all the tares.

That is the work of the angels at the Second Coming. Yet church discipline is a sort of firstfruits in that process. Paul wrote to Timothy,

> The sins of some people are evident, directing you to your judgment of them, but the sins of others follow later (1 Timothy 5:24).

It is with reference to those whose sins become apparent that church discipline deals. It is not a process of separating all the tares from the wheat, but of separating from the church both tares and those who look like tares because of an unrepentant life-style. Church discipline is one of the two ways—the other being apostasy—in which the church makes a "judgment" about those who have a false profession of faith. John tells us:

> They went out from us, but they weren't of us; because if they had been of us, they would have remained with us. But this happened that it might appear that they all aren't of us (1 John 2:19).

What this means is that those who leave the church, renouncing Christ, make it evident that though at one time they were part of the visible body, they were never saved; they never belonged to the invisible church. Clearly, a genuine Christian may also leave the church in a fit of anger or in a time of crisis without renouncing Christ. If he is a genuine Christian, we may infer from John's words that he will return in repentance to the church. But unregenerate persons who were within the outward, organized church but not really "of" the inner, saved body of Christ, unless they are converted subsequently, will not return. Something like this is what happens in church discipline.

Church discipline is initiated many times when unsaved persons who are members of the visible church fall into a sin that eventually becomes evident. Because they will not or cannot change (or both), good discipline, in place and functioning smoothly, often roots them out in time. If they don't leave of their own accord during the process of discipline,[1] they must be put out of the church. One of the reasons why the modern church, though large in numbers, is so weak in power is that it harbors within its membership so many unconverted persons who, if discipline were in force, would be eliminated from the ranks.

But it is not only unbelievers who are put out of the church in the process of church discipline. Remedially—and here we come to the answer to the question posed above—contumacious believers are also removed from the church and handed over to Satan, who is used by God in His wise providence to chastise them and bring them back to Himself. That God should use Satan and the world as a whip to spank His rebellious children should be no surprise to those who are conversant with the Old Testament. Time and again that is the message of the Old Testament books.

Take, for instance, the Book of Judges. The book is a story of God's dealings with rebellious Israel who, sinning against Him, wanders away from Him only to be brought to repentance by the rigors of subjection to one or another unbelieving foe. In subjugation, Israel cries out in repentance and God raises up a deliverer. To God's glory and the enemy's discomfort, his efforts to "destroy" God's church only end in leading it back

---

[1] If a person leaves during the process of discipline, he is to be considered *as* a heathen and as a publican on the basis of 1 John 2:19. Later, by repentance, he may demonstrate that he is not, but for the time being he must be treated as such. Erasure from the church roll of such persons is equal to the removal from the midst. He should be told so, and if he persists in going "out from us," the fact should be noted in the elders' minutes.

to Him in repentance. The exile in Babylon perhaps even more closely approximates the fifth step of church discipline. In exile—in the kingdom of darkness—God taught His people to repent and flee idolatry.

"AS A HEATHEN AND A TAX COLLECTOR"

The final word of Christ concerning the process of church discipline, found in Matthew 18:17b, is,

> And if he refuses to listen to the church, treat him as a heathen and a tax collector.

The heathen was outside the church; he had never been a part of it. The tax collector was a Jew who had been put out of the church because of his collaboration with the enemy and because of his theft. The person who is put out of the church, handed over to Satan, and thus no longer to be considered a believer is to be treated exactly as one would treat other unbelievers. This means that, while making no *final* judgment about his actual heart condition, the church is to treat him *as if* he were an unbeliever.[2] He gives no evidence of being a believer since he refuses to heed the authority of Christ vested in His officers in the church. The church does not judge his heart (God alone is the Heart Knower), but it must judge his words and actions. By word and action he has acted "as a heathen and tax collector" does and must be treated as one. The judgment is a *functional* one, that is to say, the church in all her relationships to him functions as it does toward an unregenerate person.

---

[2] In the same way that an unbeliever within the church who is undergoing discipline is treated "*as* a brother" during step 4 (cf. 2 Thessalonians 3:15).

It is possible that the individual whom you remove, being a believer in rebellion, will repent and return. This is what happened with the incestuous man in Corinth who, after he was put out, repented of his sin and was restored to fellowship in the church. The repentant believer too must be restored (see chapter 9 for the process of restoration). But until and unless he does so, he must be treated exactly as you would treat an unbeliever.[3] That means to say, for example, that if he wishes to marry a believer, you may not permit it, since believers are to "marry only in the Lord" (1 Corinthians 7:39). That also means that when you talk to him you have an obligation to evangelize him. You meet him after he has been removed from the church. Here is a slice of your conversation:

"And John, let me tell you something important that you ought to know about. The Bible says we are all sinners who need a Savior. That's why Christ came into this world. He ..."

"Hey, wait a minute! What are you trying to do, evangelize me?"

"Well, as a matter of fact, yes."

"Well, let me tell you a thing or two. I may have been put out of the church, but I'm still a Christian."

---

[3] Laney is wrong when he advocates the possibility of disciplining someone who is not a member of the church. He calls the "absence of official church membership" a "mere technicality" (p. 154). Church membership was so important that Paul and Silas baptized the Philippian jailer into the membership of Christ's church *at midnight* with Paul's back still bloody from a beating! He did not even wait till morning! Identification with Christ's church is important; without it, one *must* be treated "*as* a heathen and publican."

"I have no reason to think so. You refused to heed and obey Christ's Word, just like an unsaved person. Now let me tell you about the gospel. . . ."

If John is a Christian, which the conversation indicates might be true, you continue to evangelize him anyway in order to bring him to a realization of his anomalous situation and to "shame" him into repentance and restoration. If he isn't a Christian, God may use your witness to bring him to Himself.

THE TERMS AND THE REALITY

In the previous chapter I tried to show that the term *excommunicate* (lit., "to put out of fellowship; disfellowship") is a more appropriate designation for step 4 than for step 5. While it is true that there is a lack of fellowship between believers and unbelievers (2 Corinthians 6:15–16) and that the disfellowshipping that began in step 4 carries over to step 5, the New Testament uses other terms and expressions to describe the dismissal of a member from the care and discipline of the church. The way the New Testament puts it is

1. Remove him from your midst (1 Corinthians 5:2);
2. Clean out the leaven (1 Corinthians 5:7);
3. Get him out of your midst (1 Corinthians 5:13);
4. Deliver this person to Satan (1 Corinthians 5:5);
5. I have handed them over to Satan (1 Timothy 1:20);
6. Treat him as a heathen and a tax collector (Matthew 18:17).

These are the ways in which the New Testament describes the actions that terminate one's membership in the visible, organized church. Three actions can be found in these expressions: (1) removing, cleaning, or getting him out of the midst; (2) handing him over to Satan; and (3) treating him as a heathen—each of which emphasizes a distinct fact about his termination. The first shows the imperative for getting him out of the church (there the emphasis is on the welfare of the congregation and the honor of God's name). The second speaks of concern for the one who is removed; he is to be handed over to Satan to be "taught" and "for the destruction of the flesh so that the spirit may be saved." The third speaks of the manner in which the members of the church are to treat him—the same way they treat unbelievers.

Incidentally, since the unrepentant person whose membership in the church has been terminated is said to be "removed from the midst," some think that he is not to be allowed to attend the worship services of the church. That is a wrong reading of the passage. What Paul means is that he is removed from the care and discipline of the church; he is no longer to be considered a member of the organized church. "In the midst" means among believers, as one of them.[4] But since he is to be treated as a heathen, and since heathen are permitted to attend the services of the church (1 Corinthians 14:23–25), unless he is acting divisively he should be allowed to hear the preaching of the Word and should be witnessed to by the members, treating him like any unbeliever who enters. Perhaps God will use the preaching of the Word to bring him to repentance.

The removal formula used by Paul, "Get this

---

[4]Cf. Exodus 33:3, 5; Deuteronomy 11:6; 13:5; 17:20; 18:54; Joshua 7:13; Judges 18:20; Matthew 18:20. The phrase "in the midst" has to do with the company or community of God's people, not the physical meeting place in which they worship.

wicked person out of your midst!" (1 Corinthians 5:13), comes from the Old Testament. It occurs six times in the Septuagint in the Book of Deuteronomy: 17:7; 19:19; 21:21; 22:24; 24:7. The only difference between the formula found there and Paul's use here is that he turns the indicative of the Old Testament into an imperative because he is urging the church at Corinth to fulfill its disciplinary obligations. Because of this link between the Old and the New Testaments, it would seem that Paul is endorsing the use of this formula as a proper way of designating the act that terminates one's membership in the body. That is why I have called the chapter "Removal From the Midst."[5]

It is interesting that the New Testament adoption of this formula shows the severity of the penalty of removal. In each instance from Deuteronomy cited above, the perpetrator of the crime was to be removed from the midst and put to death! Moreover, in Deuteronomy 17:8–13, failure to *heed* the authority of the church exercised by the priest in God's name (v. 12: if he won't *"listen"*) was called "rebellion" (v. 12), and the rebellious person was to be removed from the midst and put to death. So in general, as well as in particular instances, anyone failing to heed God's authority was removed by death.

Paul's use of the Deuteronomy formula for the removal of persons from the Corinthian church shows that this act is *judicial*—the New Testament equivalent to stoning—and not merely, or even in the first place, remedial, as White/Blue as well as Laney seem to think. Removal is a serious matter, not to be taken lightly or thought of merely in terms of chastisement. That is why, particularly in step 4 but also in all earlier stages of

---

[5] That is, from the covenant community.

church discipline, it is important to set forth the danger involved in failing to repent.

It is also instructive to note that when an individual or a church failed to exercise discipline, God Himself did. In 1 Corinthians 11:17–32 we read that God struck members of the body with illness, making them weak and even taking the lives of some of them (v. 30). In this section Paul says, "If we carefully judged ourselves, we wouldn't be judged."

There is the point. When discipline is carried on faithfully, there is no need for God to intervene. "But," Paul continues, "when the Lord judges us, He disciplines us so that we shall not be condemned with the world" (v. 32). Those words sound similar to Paul's comments about delivering a person to Satan for the destruction of the flesh "that his spirit may be saved on the Lord's day" (1 Corinthians 5:5). It would seem that the two are similar concepts: Paul is saying Satan may have the dismissed brother's body (1 John 5:18 makes it clear that under ordinary circumstances, when he is under God's protection within the church community, "the evil one cannot touch" the believer); in the case of Job (who was not being disciplined), it is clear that Satan could not lay a hand on him without God's special permission.

While the "destruction of the flesh" speaks of the physical abuse by Satan of the one who is handed over (delivered) to him, there is also a remedial function to termination that comes to the fore more clearly in 1 Timothy 1:20. There Paul speaks of "handing over" Hymenaeus and Alexander to Satan "*so that they may be taught by discipline* not to blaspheme." "To blaspheme" means not only to speak lightly or profanely of spiritual things, but more generally (as here), "to rail, revile, or slander" a human being (e.g., 1 Corinthians 10:30). While these men had made shipwreck of their faith, Paul entertains the hope that the "discipline" of removal and, in particular, of being handed over to Satan will "teach" them.

So, unlike the Old Testament removal, New Testament church discipline has an additional, remedial function. We see it, of course, in the repentance and restoration of the man at Corinth.

PROCEDURES AND RECORDS

Careful records of proceedings and decisions relating to all official discipline (step 4, A and B, and step 5) should be kept. That is a part of good order. In this time when people are suing the church for obeying God, it is especially important to be able to substantiate the fact that you have followed your own procedures as they are laid down in your denominational book of discipline or in the bylaws of your congregation (and let me warn you to do so *to the letter* so that no one can fault your actions on a technicality).

Incidentally, if there are no written procedures to which members of your congregation have given approval upon coming under the care and discipline of your church, and which are made available to them at that time, it is high time for your congregation to adopt some. Presbyterian denominations have had procedures for official church discipline, and even forms for removal from the midst, that they have followed since the time of the Reformation. If you are unfamiliar with them, I suggest that you buy a copy of the *Book of Discipline* from the Orthodox Presbyterian Church, 7401 Old York Road, Philadelphia, Pennsylvania 19126, to use as a guide. In it you will find all you need to conduct church discipline in an orderly, efficient, and scriptural manner.

Let me emphasize two things at this point, however. First, when members unite with the church, they should not only make a profession of faith in Christ (that is essential), but in the light of 2 Corinthians 10:6 and Hebrews 13:17, etc., they should also agree to submit to the authority and discipline of the church, should they be found delinquent in doctrine or life.

Second, at every point but especially at the trial and dismissal from the church, complete, accurate, and detailed records should be kept of all proceedings. The conclusions and the bases on which such conclusions are made (including testimony and evidence) should be preserved in the elders' minutes book or in private files referred to in that book. Records of any registered letters sent to summon a brother who then refused to respond to them should be preserved.

While all these matters may seem to be burdensome, you will be very glad you have carefully taken the time to see to them if any problems should arise later. I shall speak further of keeping records of restoration in the next chapter. But while I am on the subject, let me also suggest that if a brother, officially disciplined at stage 4 A or B, repents, notation should be made in the elders' minutes not only of the disciplinary action and proceedings by which he was disfellowshipped (excommunicated; removed from table fellowship, but not from the care and membership of the church), but also of the fact that he was restored to fellowship, and that the matter is closed.

All these records should be kept for the twofold purpose of safeguarding the church and protecting the brother or sister who undergoes discipline. If someone should raise a matter that has been officially set to rest by the church, the restored member ought to be able to point to the records to show that the matter is closed and that it is improper to bring it up again.

MOURNING

Terminal discipline being what it is—a fearful action in which one is handed over to Satan for the destruction of the flesh—should cause the church to "mourn" for the one who is removed from the midst, even as it removes him (1 Corinthians 5:2a). The mourning should also cause the church to search its own conscience to see whether part of the fault for the problem (as in Corinth) may lay at its own feet. Did it fail to discipline properly at earlier stages? Was there lack of care all along? Was the instruction of the church adequate?

At a time like this the church, while it must not flagellate itself, should take cognizance of failures in its ministry of care and discipline, ask God's forgiveness, and determine to set things right for the future. (And where it may have failed the terminating member, it must seek his forgiveness for that specific failure; it is important to make it clear to him and any others involved that your failure does not excuse his sin and his contumacy.)[6] Such a time, as 1 and 2 Corinthians show, can be a time of great change and growth for the congregation itself.[7]

This word "mourning," or "lamenting" (*pentheo*), is used in the Beatitudes (Matthew 5:4), of the friends of the bridegroom who are not able to mourn (Matthew 9:15), and in numerous other places where people mourn over death. As the use of the Old Testament formula indicates, termination of the care and discipline of one by the church is in some sense like a funeral. The only difference is that in the Old Testament, death was the consequence of sinful, contuma-

---

[6] Indeed, your action may provide the example of repentance that he needs.

[7] Cf. especially 2 Corinthians 7:7–16.

cious action, and consequently there was no possibility of remedial repentance and restoration; in this new age (since Christ has risen from the dead) it is possible for a believer who is removed to rise from the dead metaphorically through repentance.

One never should be removed from the midst with the "good riddance" attitude that is sometimes found in churches. The so-called backdoor revival is nothing of the sort. We had better adopt the same attitude as the father who mourned for the Prodigal Son and longed for his return, scanning the horizon and running to him at first sight. It should be a solemn time of conscience-searching, mourning, and prayer when someone is removed from the midst.[8]

---

[8] Not only should the entire congregation be informed of the removal of any member, but a time of prayer and mourning probably should be set aside. At any rate, the entire congregation should be instructed about how to relate to the former member and warned about the potential dangers of not doing so.

9

Restoring to Fellowship

In the previous chapter we left the offender in the kingdom of darkness and the church mourning over his dismissal. This is a happier chapter that speaks of repentance, reconciliation, and restoration. We will talk here, not of mourning, but of rejoicing. Our concern is about what happens when the prodigal son returns home.

The process of restoration is set forth in 2 Corinthians 2. Among other things, three factors stand out:

1. The repentant offender must be forgiven;
2. He must be assisted;
3. He must be reinstated in love.

These three factors come to the fore especially in verses 6-8:

The punishment that the majority inflicted on this person is sufficient;
   so, instead of going on with that, you should rather forgive and comfort him, so that he won't be overwhelmed by too much pain.

Therefore, I urge you to reaffirm your love to him.

These are wonderful verses. The love, the concern, the tenderness exhibited in them is remarkable. Paul can be stern, but he can also be tender. In 1 Corinthians 5, his sternness is revealed; it was a time for sternness, and he did not hold back. But now, according to 2 Corinthians 2, is the time for tenderness; and he does not hold back here either.

Some had been inclined to allow the offender too much freedom, not thinking it necessary to remove him from the church. At them Paul thunders, "You are arrogant! Clean him and his leaven out!" Now, to any who would put the repentant brother on the spit and slowly turn him over the fire before accepting him back into the church, he says, "He's had enough; don't go on with the punishment. Be careful that he isn't overwhelmed by it."

This balance is rare in the church. Too often churches are weighted toward one or the other of these two extremes. To strike the proper balance is difficult.

FORGIVENESS

Since I have written extensively on the subject of forgiveness in my book *More Than Redemption,* I shall not speak about the matter in detail in this place. Moreover, I have already had something to say about forgiveness here in chapter 5. Let me remind you, therefore, that forgiveness is a promise in which one person goes on record as declaring he will never again bring up another's offense and hold it against him. The past as a debt is discharged; he is no longer held liable. His offense may be remembered only to help him to learn to act differently in the future. The offense will not be mentioned to him, or to others, and will not be the subject of brooding on the part of those who granted forgiveness.

That the matter is completely closed and should not again be raised once forgiveness is granted is an important point to emphasize to a congregation receiving back an offender who, as in the case at Corinth, may have been wallowing in heinous and disgusting sin. It will take every bit of encouragement and instruction to enable some members of the congregation to follow the proper course as presumably it did in Corinth. Doubtless, Paul was concerned about such matters when he wrote 2 Corinthians 2:6-8.

Forgiving is not the same as forgetting. Nor does the Bible command us to "forgive *and forget*." What it tells us is that our model of forgiveness is God's forgiveness of us (Ephesians 4:32). How does God forgive? He promises us, "Your sins and iniquities will I remember against you no more" (Jeremiah 31:34c).

"To remember no more" is not the same as forgetting. It is to work actively at not raising a matter; to forget is to have a matter passively fade from memory. The first is forgiveness; the latter is the result of forgiveness. One can promise not to raise a matter again and he can keep that promise, whether he feels like it or not. He cannot promise to forget. Forgiving leads to forgetting, because if a matter is never raised to anyone else and if it is not brooded upon by the one who granted forgiveness, it will soon fade from memory. I have seen even sins with the most serious social consequences, the grossest sorts of offenses, forgotten in shorter time than one would think possible when the promise of forgiveness is kept.

Forgiveness is granted upon repentance. Why

would some have hesitated to forgive? Why does Paul say to stop carrying out the punishment and forgive immediately? Probably for two reasons. First, there are always some who want to exact a pound of flesh. They cannot think that a person has suffered enough. To all such, Paul says, "It is enough. Stop it and forgive!" Second, there are always some who want to be sure the repentance is genuine. They will forgive only when they see fruit worthy of repentance. To all such, Jesus says, "And if he returns to you seven times saying, 'I repent,' forgive him" (Luke 17:4).

Note that Jesus says to forgive the person on the basis of his naked word: ". . . *saying*, 'I repent.'" You must not wait for fruit in order to grant forgiveness. The fruit will come in time—but it takes time. If after proper help and instruction there is no change and sin persists, then, when fruit should appear, you may begin to question the repentance. Indeed, this may once again lead to church discipline. But at the moment, when one comes saying that he is repentant, you must forgive him. If we are to err at this point, it must be on the side of leniency.

The church, then, must make a formal declaration of forgiveness to the repentant sinner and place on the records the fact that it has done so and that the matter is closed. All the members should receive word of the restoration in the same way that the removal was announced, and they should be instructed about how to act toward the forgiven brother or sister.[1] Any within the body who fail to forgive should be warned of the fact that to persist in such failure would place *them* in jeopardy of church discipline.

---

[1] Note that whenever the congregation as such is called upon to act in relationship to an offender (in stages 4 or 5 or in restoration), it needs to be given instruction about what to do.

ASSISTANCE

Paul writes, "Forgive and assist him" (2 Corinthians 2:7). The word for "assist" is *parakaleo*, variously translated in the New Testament as "comfort, help, assist, urge, persuade, counsel." The word, as you can see, is a very general one meaning, literally, "to call alongside for assistance." In this passage it has that very general meaning. It refers to giving the returning brother or sister whatever help—and all the help— needed to be reestablished properly in the congregation.

This assistance, or help, is too frequently missing in churches. As a result, reinstated members make their way only with great difficulty and may fall again into sin. Converted Sauls must be welcomed with open arms and hearts, because they will need much help.

What kind of help? Counseling about the problems and the sins that led to their ouster in the first place. Help in becoming reassimilated into the body. Help in making new social contacts and reinstating old ones. Help in reconciling themselves with others to whom they spoke hard words or toward whom they did despicable things. They will need guidance in finding their place in the body so that they can once again begin to use their gifts (none of this business of making them wait six months to rejoin the choir!). They may need medical assistance; Satan can be rough, and if they have been in his hands for any length of time, they will probably bear the marks that show it. They may need financial help.

I shall not try to catalog all of the possible ways in which a returning brother should be assisted; I need only to say that the church must look for those ways and offer help that is adequate.

REAFFIRMATION OF LOVE

"Reaffirming love" is an interesting phrase. The word "reaffirm" is *kurao,* a legal term that means to reinstate one to a position. It is a term that speaks of formal restoration to full membership.

The "punishment" mentioned in 2 Corinthians 2:6 is the sort of punishment that we speak of as "penalizing" a person. It means "to penalize by taking away rights and privileges." But now the church which formally stripped him of his membership by removing him from the midst must formally reinstate him, in love, as a full member. No rights and privileges of membership are to be withheld. He is not to be considered in some probationary state; he is no longer to be considered under negative discipline of any sort.[2] Of course, he is under the same requirements of the positive, preventive discipline as all the other members.

Formal reinstatement must be made as publicly as dismissal was, and in the same manner if possible. The Prodigal Son was given a robe, a ring, and a party in his honor, showing us that joy should accompany the return of the son who was lost but now is found (that is the message of the three-part parable in Luke 15). The church must be warned about the grumbling of the scribes, whose failure to rejoice was the occasion for the parable in the first place. Like the elder son, they complained and refused to rejoice over the prodigal's return. Restoration of an offender to the flock is a time for rejoicing and ought to be made such. Just as the church may have engaged in a time of mourning and set aside a time for prayer as they were forced to dismiss the brother, so too should they take

---

[2]To reaffirm *love* toward the offender is to welcome him into the full status of brotherhood in which we show him once again the *brotherly* love he lost when he was removed from the family.

time to meet together and rejoice over the return of the offender—perhaps at a dinner to celebrate the occasion and welcome him home in joy.

There is little more to say about this aspect of discipline except to remember that to preserve the gains that have been made, each of the three things listed above is essential. They will take time and commitment on the part of a number of members of the church. But, as Paul says, we must do these things "so that Satan won't be able to gain an advantage over us ..." (2 Corinthians 2:11a).

It is such efforts by the church on behalf of the returned sinner that will defeat Satan in his attempt to recapture the brother or sister who has been wrested from his grasp by the prayers of the church and the grace of Christ.

10

Cross-Congregational Discipline

So far I have been considering discipline within the local church that involves members of the same congregation. Now it is important to tackle the somewhat more complex questions of how to handle the problem of cross-congregational discipline.

Within the same denomination the ways and means for pursuing cross-congregational discipline are usually formalized in a denominational book of government and discipline. If they are not, you should work for a common Book of Discipline that provides for such measures.

What I wish to address in this chapter is the more difficult problem of how to carry on discipline among churches that are not related denominationally.

Bob and Phil, members of two Bible-believing congregations of different persuasions, have broken fellowship over a business deal. Phil, an automobile mechanic, maintains that all the work he did on Bob's car was necessary and, though he charged Bob five hundred dollars, that was a good price for the labor and parts provided; indeed, below the going rate. Bob disagrees. He thinks that Phil did unnecessary work on the car and has stuck him with a huge bill, which he refuses to pay. Bob claims that he told Phil to let him know if the cost would exceed two hundred dollars; Phil says Bob gave no such instructions. Rather, Phil maintains that Bob said, "Go ahead and do whatever has to be done," and indicated no reservations about the cost.

The matter cannot be resolved by going to court (1 Corinthians 6 forbids that).[1] But since they cannot work it out between them, the matter must be settled by the church. Bob has told a number of people at his church what a rotten deal he got and how Phil cheated him. As a result, there is evidence that Phil's business is suffering. Phil has not yet been paid.

Phil goes to his pastor for advice. The pastor says, "It seems to me that since Bob has made the matter public, it can be dealt with on that level. But why don't you take a couple of mutual friends and try once more to work out matters? If you do not succeed, go to his pastor and seek help."

One more visit is made. Phil and those with him get nowhere. Bob says he will not pay a cent more than two hundred dollars, and he refuses to discuss the issue further. Phil makes an appointment with Bob's pastor, asking him to bring the matter officially before the church. The pastor in turn suggests that all four of them talk about it; he sets a date for the conference. But nothing comes of their meeting. Both men state and steadfastly maintain their positions. Bob tries to hand Phil a check for two hundred dollars and declares that the matter is over. He wants to hear no

---

[1] God forbids believers to take other believers to court.

more about it. Phil shows the pastor receipts for parts that, apart from extensive labor costs, amount to nearly two hundred dollars in themselves. He refuses to take the check, declaring that to do so is to forfeit his right to a larger sum.

Where does the matter go from here? Regardless of how the issue turns out—which is not our concern at the moment—what steps should Phil take from here on?

Phil has two options. First, in accordance with 1 Corinthians 6:7 he can determine to accept the loss and drop the whole matter. If he does so, he must be sure he bears no resentment against Bob. In particular he must not speak disparagingly about Bob to others. If Phil drops it, it must be dropped *entirely*. (Incidentally, Phil had this option at earlier stages as well.)

But it would seem from his refusal to accept the check that Phil will want to pursue the matter further. Given his rejection of the first option, what is Phil's second? He may pursue the matter officially before Bob's church. He should inform the pastor that he is not satisfied to let the matter drop and settle for two hundred dollars, especially since he has lost five customers from Bob's church because of what he can only call slanderous gossip on Bob's part. His concern is that the church deal with his charges of theft and slander against Bob.

Before making charges of slander or gossiping, Phil must have evidence to substantiate them. This will consist not only of presenting the bills and receipts that he brought to the first conference, but also being able to call on witnesses to the slanderous statements made to others. If he can produce such evidence, he will be in a position to establish his case. Apart from evidence and witnesses, he should not proceed further (cf. 2 Corinthians 13:1).

WHAT IF THE CHURCH DEFAULTS?

All of the foregoing is rather simple and straightforward. But what if Bob's church refuses to hear Phil? What if the pastor says, "Well, Phil, I've done all I can to reconcile the two of you. In our church we don't do anything more; no, we will not discipline Bob." This possibility is not at all unlikely today.

There is no direct biblical instruction about this matter because there was no denominational problem in the first century (although there were inter-church dealings such as the council described in Acts 15). But using the approach stipulated by the words of Christ in Matthew 18, it would seem that the following procedure should be followed:

1. Phil (perhaps with the guidance of his own pastor) should gently read Matthew 18:15ff. to Bob's pastor and urge him and his church to follow the Scriptures in this matter. He should not simply go along with weakness on the part of Bob's church. Rather, in a kind but firm manner, he should insist that, since they call themselves a Bible-believing church, they are bound to do what the Bible requires. Often this sort of kind but strong pressure will prevail.

2. If that action proves to be fruitless, then (on the basis of Matthew 18) he should take someone with him (preferably his own pastor) to confront Bob's pastor. Frequently the matter will be settled at this level.

3. But suppose Bob's pastor refuses to hear them. Then, on the analogy of Matthew 18, he should "tell it to the church." That would probably mean having Phil's elders request a meeting with the elders of Bob's church. If this meeting occurs, Phil's elders may be able to persuade Bob's that this is the biblical thing to do and may be able to help them in conducting a fair

trial. The issue in points 2 and 3, please note, is not Phil's losses, but the question of whether Bob's church will follow Matthew 18. The two issues should not be confused.

4. Let us suppose, as too often is true, that Bob's elders refuse to meet or, after meeting, refuse to carry the case further. Then, short of Phil's willingness at this point to drop the whole matter, his church would seem to have but one recourse: again, on the analogy of Matthew 18, Phil's church should declare Bob's church to be "as heathen and publicans." That is to say, they should declare them to be "no church" since they will not draw a line between the world and the church by exercising discipline.[2]

This decision should never be taken unless the most careful and kind attempts have been made to try to effect proper discipline in the other church. But there must come a point at which the matter is set to rest. God will have no loose ends dangling in His church.

5. If Bob's church is declared to be no church by Phil's church, then and only then may Phil treat Bob "as a heathen and a tax collector." If he wishes to do so, Phil may now take Bob to civil court. At times this may be an unwise move, a poor testimony in a community that doesn't understand, and in some cases, even an unloving act if done in bitterness. But the practical possibility now exists. Sometimes it is wiser to drop the matter here (or earlier), and Phil always has that option.

6. If the act of declaring another church to be no church (because it will not define itself by church

---

[2] Even if Phil should wish to drop his matter against Bob, the other issue—the dealings between the two churches—should be pursued to its end. A church, declared to be no church, may be restored upon repentance.

discipline) is to be carried out, it is important to keep accurate records, testimony, etc., of all that transpired. Moreover, before doing so, the other church should be warned of the possibility of this action.

Let me suggest two variations on this theme. Where a congregation is part of a denomination, the matter should be taken through the procedures prescribed by the denominational standards before taking the step of declaring it no church. In the case of a nondenominational congregation or one in which the denomination does not function in cases of church discipline, it might be advisable to call in one or two other congregations in the community to intercede; if nothing results from this, have those congregations agree also to declare the contumacious congregation to be no church.

RESPECTING DISCIPLINE

There is another matter. Consider this scenario: Frank leaves his wife, Alice, for another woman. All efforts to bring about reconciliation fail. Frank is removed from the midst of his church. Sometime later he divorces Alice and marries the other woman. Several months after the remarriage, Frank decides to unite with another church down the street.

Frank's former pastor calls up the pastor of the second congregation and tells him that Frank was removed from the church of Jesus Christ on proper grounds by church discipline. He says, "We would rejoice if Frank is repentant and if he wants to become a part of your church. We certainly won't stand in his way. But first he has business over here. He must seek Alice's forgiveness and the forgiveness of the congregation. Until then, he isn't eligible for membership in Christ's church anywhere."

If the second pastor responds biblically, Frank will be refused membership unless he repents and does works appropriate to repentance (at a bare minimum, that means settling matters with Alice and the former congregation). But, as in many situations, let us suppose that the second church receives him anyway. Then it would seem that on the analogy of Matthew 18, the two churches must become involved to the point of satisfaction or the unchurching of Frank's new congregation by his former one.

Now, if proper procedures were in effect in the first place, such things would not happen. Whenever a stray sheep wanders into another fold, or whenever a person removed from the midst of one congregation seeks membership in another, he should be dealt with in a way that shows proper respect for the care and the discipline of the congregation to which he belongs. After all, it is difficult enough to get churches to exercise biblical discipline in the first place. How discouraging it is to find that it has been undercut by some other church down the block!

HANDLING CHURCH HOPPERS

What am I talking about? Well, first let's take up the question of the church hopper. There are times when a person should change churches, but he ought to do so for only the gravest reasons: a major change of doctrinal beliefs, apostasy on the part of the former church, or its failure to exercise discipline. Too many persons wander from church to church for superficial reasons. If the churches in a community were to draw up a procedure to deal with wandering Christians, far more wanderers would be reclaimed. It would resemble something like this interchange:

"Well, it was nice to see you in church Sunday."

"Thank you, pastor, I appreciate your visit."

"Are you new in town?"

"O no! We've lived here for about ten years."

"Then perhaps you have just become Christians or are seeking to find out how to become Christians?"

"No, we've been members of the Hilltop Church since we moved here."

"I see. Well, then you've recently had a change of belief, so you are looking for a church that is more compatible with your new beliefs?"

"No. We just got tired of going there. The people aren't so nice, and I can just tell that we're going to like it much better in your church. Why, your people were so friendly, and here you are already paying us a visit!"[3]

"Well, I'm certainly happy to hear of the friendly greeting you received, but there seems to be a problem. You know, Joe, your pastor is a Bible-believing man. He may not see everything exactly as we do here, but he is a true shepherd and you are one of his flock. If you don't have a better reason for leaving that fold, you really belong there at Hilltop and not somewhere else. If you've had difficulty with some of the people there or with the pastor, I'd be happy to set up an appoint-

---

[3]How many pastors and elders are taken in by such flattery!

ment to meet together with them and see what we can do to bring about restoration."

"Oh, I see! Well, thanks, but no thanks."

"At any rate, I'll let your pastor know we've had this talk."

This wandering sheep will try another congregation. He should be met with a similar response at each place. If this were to become the practice, there would be far less wandering; church hoppers would be required to stay and face the problems they are trying to avoid.

In some places where I have spoken about this matter, pastors have drawn up a set of guidelines to follow. Why not talk to your local ministerium about it? Even if only two or three congregations go along with the procedure, it would be a marked improvement. Indeed, even if you can get no other church to go along but you make it a practice of returning straying sheep to other shepherds, you could do much by your example to gain respect for discipline among the congregations of your community.

Obviously, if the person has wandered from a liberal church, where the pastor is a wolf in shepherd's clothing, you will do all you can to snatch him away from the clutches of that wolf. But you should always attempt to restore a sheep to a true shepherd. Besides, you get no bargain when a person leaves a church for the wrong reasons.

Consider this. I had just arrived as the new pastor of a congregation when I received a phone call from the pastor of a neighboring church. He asked,

"What can you tell me about Mr. and Mrs. So and So? I understand that they used to be members of your congregation. They've been attending here lately and want to join, but there seems to be something problematic about their past."

I responded,

"I can tell you absolutely nothing. I just arrived; I hardly know my elders' names. But I'll try to find out."

I called him back:

"I asked my elders, and they tell me that the So and Sos were disciplined by our church and removed from the midst.[4] You'd better talk to them about it. If they are truly repentant we wouldn't mind them uniting with your church, but they have unfinished business here first. We would be glad to restore them upon repentance and then, if they wish us to do so, send them by letter to your church."

"Oh!" he said. "Thanks."

I didn't hear from the pastor again, but some months later I saw him at a pastors' gathering. I asked about the So and Sos.

"Oh," he said. "We took them in anyway, and they have just split our congregation. They took half a dozen families and went to start another church."

Don't expect anything but storms when you take a Jonah into your boat!

DIVISIVE PERSONS

Let me say a word about schism. In Titus 3:10 Paul writes, "After counseling him once or twice, give up on

---

[4]Actually, at that point I was still using the word "excommunicated."

a divisive person, and have nothing more to do with him."

This is a vital direction. There should be provision to speed up the disciplinary process in cases of divisive persons. If you linger too long over the process, you may find your church divided. Paul is clear: if the divisive person does not cease his divisive ways after one or two confrontations, remove him.

In cross-congregational discipline, therefore, it is not enough to do what you can at your own church. It is essential, also, to hold other churches responsible to follow Christ's directives. When another congregation refuses to follow the discipline that Christ provided for your member and you do nothing about it, it is not only that other congregation that is lax. If you fail to make every effort to get that congregation to satisfy Christ's demands, you too are guilty, and the care of your own member is seriously lacking. If the other congregation refuses to listen to your biblical directives, then that congregation, no less than an individual believer, should be "removed from the midst."

It is imperative that all these disciplinary steps be taken—and taken with the right attitude.

LIBERAL CHURCHES?

Where you have certain knowledge that a congregation denies the essentials of Christianity, you should not send persons back. Indeed, you should do all you can to get people out of such "churches." Admittedly, many cases are borderline and not quite so clear. But in the case of a liberal church, it would seem, you have a clear obligation to pursue discipline.

In those instances in which the other congregation rightly responds by exercising discipline, you may be pleasantly surprised to discover brothers where you once wondered about them. In cases where a congregation refuses to pursue discipline on behalf of a member of your congregation and you must declare them to be "no church," the discipline issue itself is what allows you to make that statement. Either way, discipline helps sharpen the focus of an otherwise fuzzy situation.

All intercongregational discipline must be carried on with the utmost care. Special care must be taken so as not to "take sides" with members of your own congregation but, instead, to make impartial judgments based on the facts.

In cases where you disagree with the judgment of another congregation, you may have to act according to your conscience in ways that differ from that judgment—but only after it has been made perfectly clear that you appreciate that they have rendered judgment. Your reasons for departing from their judgment should be given; and just as when brothers are separated by other differences which grow out of divergent interpretations and applications of the Scriptures, you must continue to recognize the other congregation as a true church of Christ.

This is very different from declaring a church to be no church. In almost every instance, the judgment of the disciplining church should be accepted. Only in cases where the judgment involved matters of conscience should it be disregarded.

11

Encouragement

Jesus gives His church three strong encouragements for pursuing church discipline. These are found in the conclusion of the Matthew 18 passage that has formed the basis of our consideration:

> Let me assure you that whatever you bind on earth shall have been bound in heaven, and whatever you loose on earth shall have been loosed in heaven.
> Again, I tell you that if two of you agree on earth about anything they ask, it will be done for them by My Father in the heavens.
> Where two or three meet together in My Name, I am there among them.
>
> (Matthew 18:18–20)

This important passage must be discussed in closing because it is Christ's own encouragement for practicing discipline. It must have been apparent to Him that in the days to come the church would find it difficult to follow His instructions about discipline. Doubtless, that is why He appended these strong words to the commands and directions concerning the matter.

CHRIST'S PRESENCE IN THE PROCESS

To begin with, notice what Christ says in verse 20: whenever God's people meet together to deal with a matter of discipline, He promises to be with them. (Literally, this is "in their midst"; we have seen that Paul uses this expression to designate the organized church when he speaks of removing "from the midst".) It is probable, therefore, that this expression does not refer to the informal aspects of discipline, but to discipline at stages 4 and 5.

That is not to say that Christ does not work through informal discipline; everything indicates that He does. But when someone must be exposed before the body, excommunicated, or eventually put out of the church, this is a very fearful aspect of discipline, and Christ here seems to encourage the elders to go ahead and take the necessary measures. (The phrase "two or three" probably refers to those who make the decision for the whole to remove someone from the church.) Though they be few, and though much responsibility hangs on the decision of a few, He will be there, working in the process, as they prayerfully pursue His ends according to His Word.

Jesus promises to work in the disciplinary process and makes no such promise to be present and working where discipline is ignored. This is both a great encouragement and a warning. It encourages those who do practice discipline, and it confronts— even explains—to those who don't. Indeed, it may well be that many of our churches are weak and have lost their impact because they have failed to exercise the process by which Christ has determined to be present, blessing His church.

Christ's presence in the process should be mentioned whenever the situation looks discouraging. He promises to be there presumably to work to bring about His will in the case. When discipline has been properly and fully pursued in obedience to Jesus, then we may be assured that the outcome is correct. This is the encouragement that is held forth in all three promises. Of course, if the church does not pursue discipline when it should, there is absolutely no assurance that the outcome will be right; in fact, there is a strong presumption that it will not be.

ANSWERED PRAYER

Again, Christ speaks to encourage the church when He declares that the prayers of even the few who may be properly involved in church discipline will be honored. That the issue for which they are praying will be granted them means that they will not make mistakes in the process of discipline if they are faithful to pray about the issues and to follow His directions. He will answer their prayers, giving them the answer that they seek.

That means, of course, that they must ask "according to His will." When they seek the will of Christ, asking Him to bring about the right results, that is exactly what they will get—nothing less. Christ will not ignore their requests, He will not leave them to themselves, but He will be present, directing the entire affair. Verse 19, therefore, is no encouragement for holding small prayer meetings; it has to do with asking about the things pertaining to the process that Jesus outlined in verses 15–17.

HEAVEN AND EARTH

Reread Christ's words in verse 18: "Let me assure you that whatever you bind on earth shall have been bound in heaven, and whatever you loose on earth shall have been loosed in heaven." This translation differs from the King James Version and exhibits a more literal rendering of the future perfect passive verb found in the original Greek text: "... shall have been ..." It is not that heaven will abide by whatever earth does; certainly not. Rather, Christ is assuring His church that they ("the few") are only confirming outwardly what has already been determined in the heavens whenever they carry out church discipline prayerfully, in His presence, as He Himself brings about the outcome.

Even if the King James were correct, verses 19 and 20 make it perfectly plain that when carried on properly, church discipline is a process in which Christ promises to work directly to bring about the right result. So in that sense, it could even be said that heaven confirms earth's action since it is an act of the church in which Christ Himself participates. To "bind and loose" means to have authority to permit or prohibit; here it pertains to the whole process of discipline that His church exercises in His name. Christ is saying, "I give you authority to exercise discipline, permitting and prohibiting those things that I have either authorized or forbidden in My Word. You exercise My authority and heaven itself backs you up."

In all three verses, then, there is strong assurance that the church will not have to "go it alone" when properly exercising church discipline.

What stronger encouragement could a church wish? Yet churches everywhere are fearful to follow God's Word. Let me urge you to consider again, if you or your congregation hesitates to obey Christ in using church discipline: Can you really do without it? The message of verses 18–20 is that you cannot, because you cannot afford to do without Christ in the midst of your troubles! According to Revelation 3:19, Christ's loving care over the churches is evidenced in His discipline of them.

HOW TO GO ABOUT IT

Fearfully, perhaps, you say "Okay, I'm convinced. My church must begin to obey Christ and reinstitute (or introduce) church discipline. How do I begin?" That is a fair question. I should like to suggest that pastors do these things:

1. Get the matter clear in your own mind. Study and restudy this book and the Scriptures to which it refers. Be sure in your own mind about the main features of church discipline.

2. Teach your elders what the Scriptures say. Hold special classes for them on the subject, give them copies of this book, discuss questions pertaining to the matter. Work with them until they are behind you. It will be very difficult, if not impossible, to effect proper church discipline if you do not have the support of the officers of your church.

3. Begin to instruct the congregation about church discipline. Preach about it; discuss it in groups, etc. Provide each member with a set of the procedures that the church will follow when implementing the biblical commands.

4. Then and only then should you begin to look at the cases in your congregation that have been neglected over the past months and years. You should

visit such persons who have been deprived of their God-given right to be disciplined and ask for their forgiveness, confessing that the church has sinned against them by not disciplining them. After receiving forgiveness and explaining the disciplinary process, the church should urge repentance on the part of the offender once more. If he refuses, then the long-overdue process of discipline should be set in motion.

5. As new cases arise, each one should be carefully and promptly pursued according to Scripture.

6. Preaching should especially encourage the congregation to follow the process of informal discipline. When they do, the need for formal discipline will radically decrease.

CONCLUSION

You have worked your way through this volume, and you can no longer say that you have no knowledge of how discipline works. In other words, you can no longer plead ignorance. That means you are obligated to begin to follow church discipline in your congregation. Pastor, get to work today. Tell your elders that you have been reading this book and that you all need to come to grips with this matter. Elder, Christian worker, if you know your congregation is amiss, then go to the pastor and to the elders and tell them of your concern.

Where there is discipline, Christ is in the midst. Where there is none—can you expect Him to be present?

Subject Index

Scripture Index